Drama Cuts

edited by

Susan Battye

PHOENIX
EDUCATION

Drama Cuts

First published in Australia in 2010
Phoenix Education Pty Ltd
PO Box 3141
Putney NSW 2112
Australia

Phone	02 9809 3579
Fax	02 9808 1430
Email	service@phoenixeduc.com
Web	www.phoenixeduc.com

ISBN 978 1 921586 27 9

Cover design by Kate Stewart
Printed in Australia by Five Senses

CONTENTS

Introduction

The extracts from contemporary twentieth century and twenty-first century plays contained in this volume represent a cross section of plays from across a group of English speaking nations, namely the Commonwealth of Nations. Regardless of whether or not English is the first language of the playwrights, the texts have been performed and published in English. This anthology serves, therefore, to highlight shared and critical points of view about the impact and legacy of a British colonial past and present. All of the plays in this volume have been performed extensively, some by professionals on world stages, others in more modest surroundings such as village squares, school halls or classrooms.

The play extracts have been selected specifically with young people in mind and with an eye not only to the study of English literature, but also to Drama or English class performance. The selection provides extracts from 13 plays in total. Extracts from the plays included in this volume have been selected not only because of their social, political, historical and literary significance, but also because of the gripping themes they present us with related to moral and physical dilemmas. The scripts include whole group play texts as well as monologues and duologues.

Plays are written to be performed and these extracts are no exception. By allowing the voices of these characters to be heard in a classroom, we enable our students to examine the plight of people from another time, another place, or another age. Their struggles and battles live on to be reinterpreted and re-examined by a new generation of readers and actors. Through the writing we can examine not only ways of speaking and acting, but also ways of thinking about age old themes such as attitudes towards the position of women in society, unplanned teenage pregnancy, the treatment of indigenous populations by conquering races, land ownership, the impact of slavery, good versus evil, exploitation, political intrigue and incompetence, the search for identity, inter-generational battles, racial prejudice, attitudes towards work, duty to parents and the state, religious freedom, class struggle, the struggle for survival in a new world/land/ environment and post colonial attitudes.

The context in which these plays have been written and were first performed varies enormously. All of the selected plays are significant in their countries of origin for a particular reason. Most of the writers have been accorded international acclaim and their works are already included in many school or university reading lists. Two of the playwrights, who were made Nobel Laureates for their playwriting are; Wole Soyinka, from Nigeria, who wrote the tragedy, *Death and the King's Horseman* and Derek

Walcott, from St Lucia, who wrote the play based on a St Lucia folk tale, *Ti-Jean and His Brothers*.

Australian play, *Cloudstreet* by Nick Enright and Justin Monjo, is based on a much loved Australian novel by Tim Winton and together with *Summer of the Seventeenth Doll* by Ray Lawler was voted in 2009 among the top five 'best loved' Australian plays. Bruce Mason's 1950's play, *The Pohutukawa Tree* in 2009 played to sell out audiences in Auckland, New Zealand and Lynda Chanwai-Earle's 1990's play, *Ka Shue (Letters Home)* continues to fascinate students because of its groundbreaking intergenerational commentary on the position of Chinese in New Zealand.

David French's much performed play, *Leaving Home*, provides a window into the social mores of a Canadian family in the 1950's. British playwright, J.B. Priestley's, *An Inspector Calls,* is a period play set at the beginning of the twentieth century which lays the blame for the suicide of a working class girl at the door of a capitalist family. Caryl Churchill's play, *Top Girls*, for which she won an Obie Award for Best Play of the Year in 1982, examines the social cost of being a career woman within a British context.

The Indian play, *Rudali* , began life as a short story by Mahasweta Devi. In 1992 it was adapted into a play by Usha Ganguli, a leading theatre director of Calcutta, and instantly became one of the most acclaimed productions of its time. The Malaysian play, *Atom Jaya* (English translation: Atomic Big Success) by Huzir Sulaiman has been performed several times in Malaysia and elsewhere with the playwright himself taking a leading role in his political satire.

Sizwe Bansi Is Dead by white South African playwright, Athol Fugard, tackles the thorny issue of apartheid. It was awarded The London Theatre Critics award for the best play of 1974. Finally, Ugandan playwright, Mercy Mirembe Ntangaare offers us a morality play *The Man, His Son and their Donkey* which has its origins in folklore and is aimed at school audiences.

One of the reasons why plays continue to survive as a literary genre is that each generation can reinterpret their themes by placing them in a contemporary context or using new production technology to highlight aspects of the script. The fact that most of them have attracted international recognition serves to point up reasons why they deserve and continue to be studied and enjoyed.

Susan Battye

Cloudstreet

Adapted by Nick Enright and Justin Monjo
from the novel by Tim Winton

Cast

(In order of appearance)

Rose Pickles	Quick Lamb
Black Man	Fish Lamb
Sam Pickles	Doctor
Dolly Pickles	Hattie (Hat) Lamb
Chub Pickles	Red Lamb
Ted Pickles	Elaine
Lester Lamb	Wogga McBride
Oriel Lamb	

13 Speaking parts. 1 Non-speaking. Chub and Doctor may be doubled.

Setting

The scenes which occur in Part 1, Scenes 8 – 17 of the play, take place in various locations before World War II. Settings include a windowless room in an old hotel in Cloud Street, Perth, Australia, belonging to the Pickles family, the front of the hotel, a doctor's surgery, the Cloud Street kitchen, a front room in the hotel, and Quick's bedroom in Cloud Street. There is a piano and perhaps a truck.

The Extract

The unruly Pickles family has inherited a hotel in Cloud Street, Perth from Sam Pickles' uncle Joel. The house has a dark history which impacts not only on the Pickles family but also on the church going Lamb family, who rent half the house. Unlike Sam Pickles, who relies on luck to get him out of trouble, the Lamb family believes in hard work. When Fish Lamb, who has suffered a near death experience, explores the windowless room in the middle of the house, he meets Rose Pickles and the fortunes of the two families become entwined.

Scene 8

[*ROSE explores the room, which is shadowed by ghosts of the house. She sees a piano.*]

BLACK MAN Once upon a time there was a big house owned by a respectable white woman who had cheated several people to get it. But the local Anglican minister believed there is good in every heart, and it only needs to be nurtured. He put a proposition to her: 'Why not make your house a mission for young native women? Then all of Perth would remember you with gratitude.'

She filled her house with black girls. She aimed to make ladies out of them so they could set a standard for the rest of their sorry race. She showed them how to serve at table and how to wear hats in church, and she locked them in at night. The girls climbed into bed with one another and cried. They had been taken from their families and were not happy. They crawled out of windows but were tracked down and brought back.

One night one young girl went into the library, a room that had no windows. There she drank ant poison and died. The widow kicked out the rest of the girls and burned their linen under the fruit trees in the backyard.

A few weeks later she was at the piano when her heart stopped. Her nose hit Middle C. That's how the minister found the woman. Her smell knocked him over like a shot from a .303. The house was boarded up and it held its breath. Until today, no-one ever lived in it again, though some swore they could hear Middle C ringing from it at night.

[*ROSE hits Middle C. She feels the presence of the ghosts and flees the room*]

Scene 9

[*SAM hangs a sign– ROOMS TO RENT– on the front of Cloudstreet. DOLLY watches, smoking.*]

DOLLY Two thousand quid down the dunny. More dough than we'd ever seen in our lives. We're poor again, dammit, shitpoor with a house as big as a church that we can't bloody sell.

SAM I always come out even...

DOLLY You're on a losing streak, Pickles, and it'll last as long as your life.

[*CHUB, TED and ROSE come home from school.*]

TED	Hey, the door of my room's locked!
DOLLY	'Cause it's not your room anymore. You'll be in with Chub.
TED	Rather sleep with you, Ma.

[*DOLLY hoots, ruffles his hair*]

CHUB	They're all locked. All this side.
DOLLY	Your father's had an idea! He's renting out half the house. I'm going to be a friggin' landlady. Twenty years. I'm too young to be tied down like that. Twenty friggin' years.
TED	That's our friggin' luck. House and no money.
CHUB	Ponds and no fish.
TED	Trees and no fruit.
CHUB	Arm and no hand.
ROSE	Oh, you're a pair of real cards. Real funny blokes.
TED	I reckon this is a friggin' house of cards. And guess who's the bloody joker?

[*DOLLY, TED and CHUB go inside the house. ROSE finds her father dividing the house in two.*]

ROSE	What's all this?
SAM	Bet you never thought you'd be a landlord's daughter, Rosebud.
ROSE	A person like you shouldn't even say the word bet.

Scene 10

[*The LAMBS arrive at Cloudstreet, perhaps in their old truck piled with furniture. ORIEL has a newspaper.*]

LESTER	You sure this is it?
ORIEL	Last on the page. Number One Cloud Street. Go on, Lest. Go in and tee it up. The kids are exhausted. Tell them what we want.

[*LESTER heads towards the front door.*]

QUICK	Looks flamin' haunted.
ORIEL	We'll be haunting it from now on. But don't worry. We're not here to stay, kids. This is just temporary. Till we get back on our feet.

[LESTER knocks. DOLLY opens the door.]

DOLLY   Yeah? Sorry, mate, we're not buyin' nothin'. Try up the street a bit. You're as white as a ghost.

LESTER   It's limestone dust. We came up from the country. Margaret River.

DOLLY   Knew a bloke from there once. Had hair growin' out his nostrils.

LESTER   It's about the house...

DOLLY   Right. I'll get the hubby. Sam? Sam! Come down here, Sam. Stop buggerizin' about!

LESTER   My name's Lester Lamb.

[SAM appears.]

DOLLY   His name's Lester Lamb.

[SAM offers his left hand.]

SAM   Come and have a look. You get half the house, half the yard, your own dunny. The corridors are everyone's, same as the stairs. Bloody big joint, eh?

LESTER   I got six kids.

SAM   Catholics, eh?

LESTER   No. No, nothin'.

SAM   Can youse pay?

LESTER   We'll pay.

SAM   You'll do. *[He sees ORIEL with the KIDS.]* My name's Pickles. Sam Pickles. It's gunna sound like a counter lunch, Lamb and Pickles. Well, bring 'em in.

[ROSE, CHUB and TED watch ORIEL directing as the LAMBS unpack and move into their half of the house.]

ROSE   Gripes, and I thought *we* looked like reffos.

TED   Three girls. Whacko!

CHUB   There's three boys, too.

TED   One's a slowbo.

ROSE   Is not.

TED   Betcha.

[SAM joins them.]

Who are they?

SAM	They're called the Lambs.
TED	God, we're livin' with sheep!
SAM	This is their half now. They pay rent, so keep away. Time for youse to be in bed. You got school tomorrow.
CHUB	I'm not going to school.
SAM	Get to bed.
	[*TED and CHUB go.*]
ROSE	You shouldn't have done this.
SAM	Shut up. I'm your father.
	[*They see FISH LAMB staring at them.*]
FISH	Mister... who stoled your fingers?
	[*QUICK comes for him.*]
QUICK	Come on, Fish. [*To SAM*] Sorry.
	[*He leads FISH away. ROSE stares at them.*]
SAM	Who stoled your fingers? That's a good one, eh?
	[*ROSE goes. SAM surveys his stump.*]

Scene 11

[*Night. FISH moves into the windowless room. He plays a note on the piano and the GHOSTS swirl above him. FISH can see them.*]

FISH	G'day. I'm Fish. Fish Lamb. Who are you?

[*The GHOSTS whisper in his ears. FISH reacts to the private story.*]

No. Sad. Sad.

[*ROSE appears in the doorway, unseen, and watches FISH. She doesn't see the GHOSTS.*]

ROSE	I could read you stories. [*The GHOSTS leave FISH.*]
	I like reading. Do you like stories?
FISH	Where are the ladies?
ROSE	This room gives me the creeps.

[*QUICK comes in and finds them.*]

It's funny. Dad's divvied up all the rooms, but nobody gets this one. He calls it No Man's Land. Don't you reckon it smells? Or is it just that it's got no windows? Ted reckons you're a slowbo. I think you're beautiful.

[*She sees QUICK and hurries away.*]

QUICK   Hear that, Fish? She reckons you're beautiful. Come on, back to bed, mate.

FISH   See the lady?

[*QUICK leads him away from the room.*]

QUICK   That's just the girl from the other side.

FISH   No. The lady. Look.

[*QUICK puts FISH to bed, then climbs in and goes to sleep.*]

Can you hear it. Quick? The ladies are fighting. The house is sad. Can you hear it?

Scene 12

[*LESTER and ORIEL are by themselves.*]

LESTER   Quick's looking blue.

ORIEL   Well, that's natural enough.

LESTER   Blames himself, thinks we blame him.

ORIEL   Don't we?

LESTER   It wasn't his fault. Why would it be?

ORIEL   But we blame him. And I blame you. And God.

LESTER   It scares me, hearing you talk like that.

ORIEL   Me too. I can't help it. I'm a sinner, Lest.

LESTER   What about Fish? What are we going to do with him?

ORIEL   We'll give him the gentlest life we can. We'll make it the best for him we know how.

LESTER   Orry? You think we should... take him to a doctor?

ORIEL   I'm not too chuffed about doctors, Lester. Neither are you.

LESTER   I know, but–

ORIEL   Hard work and plenty of food, that keeps the quacks away. And a bit of care. We'll do our best for Fish, and that's that.

LESTER   Please, Orry...

Scene 13

[*Surgery. A DOCTOR stares down FISH'.s throat with a light. FISH giggles. ORIEL sits with QUICK. LESTER puts his hands on FISH's shoulders as the DOCTOR examines him.*]

DOCTOR	What's your name, boy?
ORIEL	Fish Lamb. Samson.
FISH	Fish.
DOCTOR	Mrs Lamb, I'll ask and he'll answer.
ORIEL	Very well.
DOCTOR	Why do they call you Fish?
FISH	It's the name.
LESTER	We called him Fish, 'cause of his wit, his alertness, Doctor.
DOCTOR	Hmm. How old are you. Fish?
FISH	Nine.
ORIEL	Ten next month.
DOCTOR	Mrs Lamb! [*To FISH*] Can you count to nine?
FISH	Nine.
DOCTOR	Yes.
FISH	I'm big.
DOCTOR	Indeed. Fish, where do you live?
FISH	In the family. With Quick, Lestah...
DOCTOR	Who is this?
FISH	Lestah! My da.
DOCTOR	And who is this, Fish? Who is this lady? Fish?
	[*Silence.*]
ORIEL	Lester, he doesn't see me.
DOCTOR	Who is she, Fish?
LESTER	Please, Doctor, this –
FISH	The water.
DOCTOR	Queer. How long was he under the water?
LESTER	A few minutes. He was caught up under the net and my lamp went out –

DOCTOR	Yes. And you revived him, Mrs Lamb?
ORIEL	Yes. And I prayed.
FISH	The water.
DOCTOR	And you didn't take him to a doctor, or a hospital?
LESTER	We thought he was better. A miracle, you know.
DOCTOR	Hmm. Like Lazarus? Jesus wept.
ORIEL	But he's retarded. We had to potty train him again, start from scratch.
DOCTOR	You mean, he's improved?
LESTER	A bit, yes.
DOCTOR	A boy would have more than this regression after an experience like that.
ORIEL	Are you saying we're liars?
DOCTOR	Mrs Lamb –
ORIEL	I am a woman whose word has been respected as long –
LESTER	Oriel! –
DOCTOR	This boy seems traumatised. Are you sure he hasn't been through a great shock of some kind?
LESTER	He's been alive and he's been dead. One of those was bound to be a shock.
DOCTOR	You should think about a specialised home for him...
ORIEL	There's no home as specialised as mine, Mister!
	[*She takes hold of FISH.*]
FISH	Lestah! Lestah!
DOCTOR	Mrs Lamb, sit down.
ORIEL	Come on, Lester.
DOCTOR	Fish, where do you want to go?
FISH	The water, the water!
	[*ORIEL bundles FISH out of the office.*]
	Fast! Fast!

Scene 14

[*Cloudstreet kitchen. All the LAMBS are there. RED spins the knife while ELAINE and HAT watch.*]

HAT	This is for who washes up tonight!
RED	And this week! All this week!
ELAINE	The knife never lies, you know. It always knows best!
FISH	I wanna play! Come on, Lestah! Quick!
LESTER	It's slowing down! It's you, Hat.
HAT	Nah, got plenty in it yet. It's you, Dad.
LESTER	Nope. It's gonna be Quick. Look at him. He's getting out the tea-towel already, aren't you, mate? Here it comes again.
RED	Elaine!
ELAINE	Wait. Wait!
QUICK	Oh, God!
HAT/ ELAINE / RED	Quick! Quick! Quick gets the dishes.
LESTER	The knife never tells a fib, but it can make a bib for a squib. Here's one. Who's got a pimple on their dimple?

[*Laughter as he spins the knife again.*]

Who will it be? Round and round and round it goes, and where it stops...

RED	It's... it's Elaine. Pimple up your dimple, Ee!
ELAINE	It's not!
HAT	Carn, Ee, fair cop!
QUICK	Yeah, the knife doesn't lie!
LESTER	You kids wash up. I'll just be a tick.

[*The KIDS go.*]

We're making something here, love, I can feel it.

ORIEL	We need things.
LESTER	Plenty.
ORIEL	Don't smile me down, Lest.
LESTER	There's money left, love. We're not hungry.

ORIEL	We need work.
LESTER	I've been thinking some more.
ORIEL	Thought I smelt burning rubber.
LESTER	Thinking about this place.
ORIEL	Don't bother. It's time we were moving on. We need our own bathroom. We need a stove, the kids need clothes. They go to school like they haven't got a mother. This place is only temporary. We need to find somewhere permanent.
LESTER	Hang on. I've cottoned onto something. There's no corner shop this side of the railway line.
ORIEL	I know. I've carried the groceries back from Subi.
LESTER	I've brained it out. We could do it.
ORIEL	What are you talking about?
LESTER	A shop. Our shop.
ORIEL	Is this another one of your–?
LESTER	This is a good one, Orry.
ORIEL	Don't be a fool, Lest. We can't pay rent on a shop.
LESTER	We already are. Right now.
ORIEL	What've you done?
LESTER	I've used my noggin.
ORIEL	Explain.
LESTER	We'll use that front room for a shop.
ORIEL	Across the corridor, they'll chuck all whatsemame about it.
LESTER	They're broke, darl. They're poor as us. And lazy. Look at them, waiting for the boat to come in. They need the money. We'll pray about it. We'll take it to the Lord. No, wait on... [*He spins the knife.*] The knife never lies. If it points to me it's a Yes. To you, it's a No.
	[*They watch the knife spin. It points to LESTER.*]
ORIEL	How do you know it never lies?
	[*LESTER looks towards the MUSICIAN who watches the scene.*]
LESTER	What'll it be?
ORIEL	Somethin' I don't know. Play me somethin' I don't know.
	[*LESTER breaks into a song.*]

Scene 15

[The LAMBS set the shop up. LESTER hangs out a sign:
LAMBS' MIXED BUSINESS WE'RE LOCAL, WE'RE
HONEST, WE'RE HERE. *GERRY CLAY passes in uniform,
notices DOLLY. She sees the sign.]*

DOLLY	'We're local, we're honest, we're here.' Wouldn't it turn your guts? *[To ORIEL]* Well, how's it doing, ducks?
ORIEL	Bit of a slow start. But we'll be right. If there's one thing we've got, it's stickability.
DOLLY	Stickability. How much you made so far?
LESTER	A shilling and a ha'penny.
DOLLY	Oh, you'll get rich if you keep this up.
ORIEL	And you'll have an income, Mrs Pickles. Is there anything I can get you?
DOLLY	Oh. Couple of spuds?

[LESTER gives the kids a lolly. ORIEL bags the spuds.]

ORIEL	There. That'll be –
LESTER	On the house.

[DOLLY takes the potatoes. She sees a row of cakes.]

ELAINE	Dad baked these.
DOLLY	Good for him.

[DOLLY leaves. A scream from behind the shop. HAT emerges.]

HAT	That Ted Pickles showed me his thing!

[RED picks up a pair of scissors.]

RED	Right let's get him.

[She leads the LAMB GIRLS off. DOLLY laughs, beckons to TED as ROSE and CHUB come home from school.]

DOLLY	There's my boy. Got a kiss for your old mum? *[She embraces TED.]*
CHUB	Mum, Hitler shot himself in his bunk.
TED	Bunker, Chub. Does that mean the war's over?
DOLLY	They still got to clean up the Nips, Teddy.
TED	Oh, yeah...

CHUB	What's for tea, Mum?
DOLLY	Christ knows.

[*SAM comes home, sees the shop sign.*]

SAM	What do you reckon? We're local, we're honest, we're bloody mad.
DOLLY	Least they're earning a quid. More than I can say for anyone on our side of the house. It's like this place has had a stroke, Sam. Paralysed down one side.

[*She gives ROSE the potatoes and goes.*]

ROSE	I'll get the tea on.
SAM	That's the girl.

Scene 16

[*QUICK reads a newspaper in his room.*]

QUICK   Quick Lamb reads the paper every day and sees the long lists of the missing believed killed, and the notices in memoriam for sons and fathers and brothers. The war's over, he knows, but he picks up sadness like he's got radar for it. The whole world's trying to get back to peace, but somewhere there's craters and rubble and gas chambers, and still the stories coming home as though it'll never let itself be over. 'We're lucky,' he thinks. 'The old man was too old and I was too young. We've got food, coupons, a full ration book. We're gettin' away light.'

[*ORIEL gives him food. He goes to the schoolyard.*]

Quick sees kids at school who are poor. Through the winter, Quick notices Wogga McBride. He has a queer way of eating his sandwich, hiding it under his hand. Maybe it's Quick's misery radar, but he can't *let* it be, till eventually he sees that Wogga hasn't got a sandwich at all.

[*He watches WOGGA McBRIDE pretending to eat.*]

The Lambs are patched and barefooted, but at lunchtime their mother always brings warm pies and pasties from the shop.

[*He takes food to WOGGA.*]

I'm full. Want this?

[*WOGGA runs away. QUICK watches him go.*]

Wogga lives further down the tracks towards West Perth, but he crosses at the walkway below Cloudstreet. Today is the last day of primary school, and if Quick doesn't make friends with him today, he never will. He tails him down Rokeby Road, past the football ground and up the embankment behind West Leederville station. Down beside the tracks Wogga's fooling with a stray dog that's got hold of his school bag. Quick hears Wogga laughing, even over the sound of an approaching train. Quick wants to go down and run the dog ragged with him. And then Wogga tears the bag free of the dog and sways back, shrieking with glee, and the sleeper catches his heel and he staggers and the engine smacks him with the sound of a watermelon falling off the back of a truck, and he's gone.

[*Noise and light. WOGGA disappears. QUICK runs.*]

Scene 17

[*Cloudstreet. QUICK runs headlong into his room. He finds a large stack of old newspapers. He starts to cry. FISH comes in.*]

FISH	What you laughing for, Quick?

[*QUICK stops crying, ignores FISH.*]

QUICK	Off you go, mate.
FISH	Off you go, mate. You happy, Quick?
QUICK	Go away, Fish.
FISH	You sad?
QUICK	Mate, everybody gets sad. You get sad.
FISH	When I want the water.
QUICK	What water?
FISH	The water, the water.

[*LESTER sees them together.*]

QUICK	Fish, go and play with Lon, mate. Or the girls. Go on.

[*FISH goes. QUICK is alone with the stack of old newspapers. He starts searching through them. LESTER watches.*]

Quick doesn't let himself think about what happened to Wogga. Quick thinks about nothing at all. He just hears the scissors going as he cuts out pictures, hears himself thumbing tacks into his wall. And the people in all the pictures, the burnt babies, the amputee diggers, the walking dead, they laugh at Quick, all of them, and they dance with Wogga McBride along the tracks. LESTER A lot of sad people, Quick. What are you doin' with them?

[*QUICK cuts, or puts the pictures up.*]

Knocks me round to see you like this, boy. Three days we haven't seen you downstairs. You'll starve to death. Look at these poor sods. You don't want to be like them. You don't need to be. You've got a roof over your head, family... well, we're not much, but strike... Look, come downstairs. For your mother's sake.

[*QUICK goes on cutting.*]

Well, do it for Fish. Come on. He's worried sick about you.

[*QUICK goes on cutting.*]

You know damn well your brother is busted in the head and he'll never grow up right. The least you can do is let him be happy. Don't torture him, Quick. And us. You're feeling sorry for yourself and it's making me sick. You and me understand about Fish. We were there, we were stupid enough to drown him trying to save him. You remember that. We owe him things, Quick. All we can do now is let him be happy. I can sit here and talk and get nothing back for as long as it takes to get angry enough to swat your arse and send your mother up to deal with you. But Fish, he'll wait. He'll wait till you say something to him. Don't you forget about Fish, boy. Not as long as you live, or your life won't have been worth living.

[*Silence. LESTER leaves QUICK alone. He goes on cutting.*]

Summer of the Seventeenth Doll

by Ray Lawler

Cast

(In order of appearance)

   Barney Ibbot
   Johnnie Dowd
   Bubba Ryan
   Roo Webber
   Olive Leech

5 Speaking parts. No doubling.

The Setting

The scene, which occurs towards the end of Act 2 Scene 2, takes place in the living room of a woman in her late sixties, Emma Leech, in Carlton, Melbourne, Australia, on New Year's Eve, in 1953. It is hot and the French windows are open and so is the front door. There is a front verandah, stairs leading to the bedrooms, a side board, a mantle-piece, and a chaise longue or sofa covered in chintz material. The room is a riot of colour provided by the Queensland souvenirs consisting of sixteen kewpie doll sticks, stuffed North Queensland birds, tropical butterflies on black velvet framed pictures and postcards from Queensland. The seventeenth kewpie doll has pride of place. The light that enters the room is filtered by the tangle of undergrowth outside.

The Extract

Barney Ibbot, aged forty, and Roo Webber, aged forty-one, are on their annual 'fun filled' visit to Emma Leech's house for the sugar cane cutters' lay-off season. They are experts at avoiding commitment. Olive Leech, aged thirty-nine, lives in the house with her mother Emma. Their next door neighbour is Bubba Ryan, aged twenty-two is also a regular visitor to the house in the off season. Pearl Cunningham, a widow, is also resident in the house and is caught up in the events. The boss of the cane cutting gang, Roo has arrived with a bad back and no money unlike his mate, Barney. When Roo's arch rival, cane-cutter, Johnnie Dowd, aged twenty-five, shows up unannounced at Emma's house, the scene is set for a real battle.

BARNEY	[*Drawing BUBBA into the room*]
	Here's the one I want you to meet. Bubba Ryan.
DOWD	How are yer?
BARNEY	[*Standing behind her*] Oh, she's fine ...aren't yer, kid? You see this feller? Know where he comes from?
	[*She shakes her head.*]
	Way up north where the sugar grows. And you want to know somethin' else? He's one of the best cutters and . . .
	[*BUBBA's face lights with interest.*]
DOWD	All right, Barney, don't lay it on. [*Holding out his hand*] Dowd's the name, Miss - Johnnie Dowd.
BARNEY	See - he says it just as if it meant nothin' at all.
BUBBA	[*Shaking hands slowly*] How d'you do?
BARNEY	Natural as they make 'em. [*Whispering in her ear*] The sort of fella any girl'd love to have take her to the races.
BUBBA	Races?
BARNEY	[*Rushing her off her feet*] Yeah. Tomorrow afternoon. Roo 'n' Olive, Pearl 'n' me, and you 'n' Johnnie! Whaddya say?
BUBBA	[*Confused*] Well, I dunno.
BARNEY	Oh, now, Bubba, you're not gonna be a hangout, are you? Where else can you go Sat'day afternoon?
BUBBA	Well–
BARNEY	There y'are then. Here's a chance to make whoopee. How about it?
	[*He eyes her anxiously. She looks timidly towards DOWD and then nods.*]
BUBBA	All right. If you really want me.
BARNEY	[*Triumphantly*] Easy as pie, everythin' settled.
DOWD	[*Dourly*] Not for me it ain't.
BARNEY	[*Turning*] Why, what else is there?
DOWD	I don't take things as easy as that.
	[*BARNEY opens his mouth to protest, DOWD cuts in firmly.*] You wait outside a minute.
BARNEY	But Johnnie –
DOWD	You wait outside.

[*BARNEY eyes him questioningly for a second, then hunches his shoulders and moves unsteadily out to sit on the front verandah. Inside, DOWD, not so sure of his ground now, addresses himself to BUBBA.*]

What I mean is, I know this Barney, how he rushes people and the − the things he puts over. I want to give you a chance. You don't like the idea of goin' to the races with me, you tell me now.

[*He pauses, but BUBBA waits far further enlightenment and he is forced to stumble on.*]

You won't have to worry over what he'll say, I'll fix that.

BUBBA	But I'd like to go to the races.
DOWD	You looked to me as if you were holdin' back a bit.
BUBBA	It was the surprise, that's all. Roo and Barney. they've never brought anyone from up north here before.
DOWD	[*Looking around*] I know. They've sat pretty tight on this joint, haven't they? D'you live here?
BUBBA	No, I'm from next door.
DOWD	Oh. That makes it a bigger hide than ever, then.
BUBBA	What?
DOWD	Him askin' you to go out with me.
BUBBA	No, it isn't. Not really. I been comin' in here a long time.
DOWD	Have yer? [*Glancing over the room*] Funny thing. I imagined this place pretty often. [*In answer to her puzzled look*] Oh, of course I've never been here, it's just the reputation that's been built up among the boys. I reckon you could say it's almost famous up north.
BUBBA	Things Barney said?
DOWD	Yeah. And bits of talk the boys picked up. Or made up, by the looks of it. [*He eyes the souvenirs disparagingly.*]
BUBBA	[*Nervously*] It's not a − a big place.
DOWD	Size is nothin'. It's the other things − like all the fun they're supposed to have here. I just can't see it.
BUBBA	[*Defensively*] You don't know.
DOWD	No? You tell me then.
BUBBA	[*Turning away, shakily*] H-how can I? All that's happened in a house makes a feeling − you can't tell anyone that. It's between people.

DOWD	Oh. [*Indicating the dolls on the mantelpiece*] What are the dolls in aid of?
BUBBA	Roo gives one to Olive every year when he arrives. Like a mascot.
DOWD	[*Snorting in coarse amusement*] Dolls? Is that the best he can do?
	[*BUBBA flinches.*]
	You didn't like me sayin' that, did you?
BUBBA	No.
DOWD	What are you, relation or something? [*She shakes her head.*] What's the matter then? I've hurt you some way.
BUBBA	[*Turning on him*] You shouldn't have said that about the dolls. They mean something to Olive and Roo, it's – it's hard to explain. You wouldn't understand it.
DOWD	[*Summing up her reaction, and asking her directly one of the big questions of his life*] Tell me something will yer? Why is it every time I come across anything connected with Roo, I'm supposed to act like I was too young to live up to it?
BUBBA	[*All of a sudden touched by the coincidence of then youthful insecurity*] I don't know. Maybe it's like the walking-sticks.
DOWD	The what?
BUBBA	The lolly walking-sticks. They're a sort of present – a joke we have every year when they come down.
DOWD	Beats me. [*Abandoning the puzzle*] Anyway, what's it matter, tomorrow's the thing. That is, if you'll still come with me alter the cracks I've made. Will you?
BUBBA	Yes. I'd – like to.
DOWD	What did he say your name was again?
BUBBA	Bubba Ryan.
DOWD	Bubba? Is that what they call you? [*As she nods*]
	Seems to me they're keeping you in the cradle, too. [*They look at one another in a moment of perfect understanding.*]
	What's your real name?
BUBBA	[*Softly*] Kathie.
DOWD	Kathie? Well, that's what I'll call you. Okay?
	[*He smiles at her and she responds. Then, with a rather*

*manufactured briskness, to prevent too sudden an
entanglement.*]

Hey, look at the time! I'll have to be shiftin'. [*Moving up to
the arch and calling*] Barney! [*Warmly, to BUBBA*] We'll let
him make all the arrangements, eh?

| BUBBA | Try to stop him. |

[*BARNEY re-enters the house from the front verandah.*]

DOWD   Look, I'm goin'. I told the boys I'd be at the London by seven.
Past that now.

BARNEY   Righto. You'd better say goodbye to him first.

[*DOWD moves towards the front door as BARNEY yells
upstairs.*]

Roo. Johnnie's goin' now. [*Turning back*] Everything
settled?

DOWD   Yeah. We're relying on you to fix the details.

BARNEY   [*Earnestly*] You leave it to me. I'll meet you Young and
Jackson's tomorrow morning half past ten; by then I'll have
it all lined up. Eh?

DOWD   Fine. [*Smiling over at BUBBA*] And you'll tell Kathie?

BARNEY   Kath – ? [*Following the line of Dowd's gaze and
realizing*] Oh yes, yes. Course I will.

[*ROO comes downstairs, towel over his shoulder, face half
shaved.*]

Ah! [*Brightening mechanically*] Johnnie's got to go now, Roo.

ROO   I heard yer.

DOWD   Well, hooray, Roo, I'll see you tomorrow

ROO   Yeah.

DOWD   Any message you want me to give the boys?

ROO   Oh...you know...just give 'em all the best.

DOWD   'N' tell 'em to keep out of mischief, eh?

[*There is a general polite laugh. BARNEY claps DOWD on
the back.*]

BARNEY   C'mon, I'll see you to the gate. [*As they move off*] You know
the way back? The best thing you can do is go down to the
corner; and if you don't pick up a cab by the time a tram
comes, grab that, it'll take you into the city in about five
minutes.

[They exit. ROO's stare turns to BUBBA, who is watching DOWD off through the window.]

ROO	What are you doing here, Bub?
BUBBA	Barney brought me in.
ROO	To meet him?
BUBBA	Yes.
OLIVE	*[Entering quietly through the arch]* Has he gone?
ROO	Yeah. Made quite a picnic of it, got Bubba in to meet him too.
OLIVE	'Lo darl. *[Cautiously]* Didn't seem such a bad sort of kid, really.
DOWD	I'm not blamin' him. This is Barney's doin', he cooked this up.
OLIVE	Well, it doesn't matter much, anyway, does it?
ROO	*[Facing her with repressed anger]* Olive, you dunno what he's done. He's forced me – brought Dowdie right into this house in the lay-off and forced me to – to knuckle under to him.

[He halts, unable to express his frustration.]

OLIVE	All right. You know best. Only don't make things any worse than they are. I've already got Emma moanin' in the kitchen, and Pearl bawlin' her eyes out upstairs. That's enough to handle.
ROO	What's wrong with Pearl?
OLIVE	*[Laying the tablecloth, BUBBA helping her]* Oh, you can't make head or tail of it. Something about Barney asking her to send her daughter to the races tomorrow.
BUBBA	*[Abruptly]* He didn't ask her, he asked me.
OLIVE	To go to the races?

[BUBBA nods and OLIVE laughs.]

Aah – kittens! It's all fellers – Barney wouldn't take a girl to the races with a crowd of fellers. He's havin' a loan of yer.

BUBBA	He's not. And it isn't all fellers, it's just us. Us – and Johnnie.

[OLIVE shoots a glance at ROO.]

ROO	Us and Johnnie? Did he tell you that?
BUBBA	Yes.

ROO	The two of them had it arranged before you came in?
BUBBA	Well, Barney asked me first, and then Johnnie.
ROO	[*Seething*] As thick as thieves! [*To OLIVE*] Now d'yer see? Workin' it out between them bloody bosom pals, that's what they are. Well, that's the finish. [*Hastily throwing his towel to OLIVE and moving towards the front door, yelling*] Barney! Come in here!
OLIVE	[*Following and temporising*] Maybe they've got it all mixed up.
ROO	No, they ain't. I know what his game is now. You two get out of this, down the back some place. . .
	[*BARNEY enters from offstage and weaves his way on to the verandah, where he pauses for a moment at the sound of the angry voices.*]
BUBBA	[*Frightened*] Roo...
OLIVE	I won't have any fightin', do you hear? Argue if you want to, but no fightin'.
ROO	You stay out of it.
OLIVE	Roo...
ROO .	[*Roaring*] Get out!
	[*She exits hastily with BUBBA. BARNEY appears in doorway. ROO grabs him by the lapels of his coat and hawks him inside, with a savage exclamation.*]
BARNEY	Now, easy on, Roo, I'm a bit full.
ROO	[*Shaking him, in a low voice of fury*] Don't you try and put that drunk stunt over on me. I know you had to have beer to get you through what you've done, but I know how much you've had. *I know!*
	[*With a powerful heave, he sends BARNEY across the room towards the mantelpiece. BARNEY staggers and then recovers his balance, faces ROO. His drunkenness drops from him like a cloak.*]
BARNEY	[*White-faced*] All right. So I brought Dowdie.
ROO	[*Advancing*] Yes. You brought Dowdie And don't think I don't know the reason why.
BARNEY	For your own good.
ROO	Liar! Filthy, upjumped, rotten liar!
BARNEY	[*Nettled*] Now, let me get a word in –

ROO   A man oughta cut your tongue out. [*BARNEY turns from him with disgust.*]

And the way you did it ... you just had to show him how low I'd sunk, let him see me covered in stinkin' paint.

BARNEY   What are you suddenly, a flower or somethin'? He's seen you in the fields, nearly naked, black as pitch...

ROO   [*Fiercely*] Yes, and so was he. Both of us sloggin' it out under the sun! Are you tryin' to say it's the same thing as this a job in a paint factory? Are you? Anyway, there's more to it than that.

BARNEY   [*Turning away*] Ah, there's no use talking to you...

ROO   Well, you're guunna talk. Not them lies and excuses and ... and lies of yours, this time we'll have it fair dinkum for once!

BARNEY   [*Rounding on him*] Righto then, here it is! You're so blind jealous of young Dowd I reckon you ought to get yourself looked at before it's too late.

ROO   [*Suddenly still*] Go on.

BARNEY   [*Knowing he has gone too far but unable to retreat*] That's all. And I'm not the only one says so!

ROO   Who else?

BARNEY   The boys. They weren't too pleased when you walked out on them up there, y'know. They weren't pleased at all. And I'm drummin' yer, you don't pull your socks up pretty quick, you're gunna find next season that our mob have got a new ganger for keeps.

ROO   Dowd!

BARNEY   Yeah, Dowd!

ROO   [*Deceptively quiet*] And that's why you brought him here, eh? So's I could make it up with him and get back on top with the boys?

BARNEY   Course it is.

ROO   [*Springing the trap*] Maybe you thought I could turn the trick at the races tomorrer, on a little party cooked up between you and Dowd – with Bubba as a bait!

BARNEY   [*Quickly*] Oh, that. I – I was makin' a switch.

ROO   [*Explosively*] You was makin' a switch right enough! Your money's runnin' out, you know you can't put the bite on me any more, and so here's the new champion, all loaded and ready. And it wasn't enough to chase after him up north after I walked out on the gang, now you're aimin' to get him in here for the lay-off as well.

BARNEY   [*Dangerously*] You reckon I'd work a point like that?

ROO   You'd do that and worse. 'Coz you're a slimy little leech that won't even drop off when it's got its belly full.

          [*BARNEY charges him with a roar. ROO grapples with him wholeheartedly and swings him out on to the back verandah. A confused melee of crashing pot plants, blows, and swaying ferns ensues, only part of it visible. OLIVE rushes in, followed by EMMA, BUBBA and PEARL.*]

OLIVE   Roo, stop it; stop it, Roo.

EMMA   Keep away from them, Olive.

OLIVE   [*At the French windows*] You want to murder him?

EMMA   Pair of flamin' larrikins!

OLIVE   [*Moving out of sight on the verandah*] Let him go. Roo!

EMMA   You wanna fight, why don't you get out in the street?

OLIVE   Roo!

          [*The above lines are overlapped for the effect of agitated violence, dominated by the last screaming of ROO's name. He now comes back into view, breathing heavily, but unmarked. PEARL and BUBBA watch, white-faced and scared, as he moves into the room.*]

EMMA   Lucky I didn't go straight for the cops.

          [*OLIVE appears with BARNEY. He has obviously had the worst of the encounter. OLIVE assists him down to an armchair, then speaks tremblingly to ROO.*]

OLIVE   Any more of that and the two of you will sleep out in the gutter for the night. Men your age, you oughta have more sense. What do you think you're up to, anyway?

ROO   [*Controlled*] This is no business of yours, Olive.

OLIVE   [*Her temper stirring*] Oh, I'm s'posed to sit out in the back while you kick one another to pieces, I s'pose' [*To ROO*] And why? All because you had one' rotten season up north.

ROO   It ain't that at all.

BARNEY   It is. [*Swaying to his feet*] Why don't you be a man and admit it?

OLIVE   [*Sharply*] Who wants him to admit it? It doesn't matter.

BARNEY	[*Inflamed*] Oh yes, it does. Would he have walked out on his own gang if it hadn't mattered?
	[*To ROO*] Come on. You wanted me to be fair dinkum about Dowd, let's see you square off the same way.
OLIVE	[*Angry and puzzled*] What do you want him to say − that Dowd did a better job than he did?
BARNEY	[*Straight on the nail*] Yes.
OLIVE	Righto. Roo had a bad back. Next season when he goes up, his back'll be better, and he'll beat Dowd.
	[*BARNEY gives a mechanical 'Ha ha ha' of derision. OLIVE snaps.*]
	What's so funny about that?
BARNEY	Ask him. He'll tell you.
ROO	No, I think that's up to you.
	[*He charges across at BARNEY, pushing OLIVE out of the way. He savagely whips BARNEY's arm up behind his back, and forces him to his knees, facing the women.*]
	It's your lie − you tell 'em!
BARNEY	[*His face contorted with pain*] Aah − cut it out.
ROO	[*Increasing the pressure*] Tell 'em.
BARNEY	[*Gasping*] He...he never had a bad back.
	[*Still holding him ROO speaks over his head to the women through gritted teeth.*]
ROO	Did you hear that? No strain, nothin'. Dowd did a better job than me because he's a better man than I am. That's what he wanted you to know!
	[*He shoves BARNEY forcibly from him and the smaller man spins around on the floor, grasping his arm and crying out from an indefinable sense of loss and repentance.*]
BARNEY	You damned fool - do you think I would have told them?
ROO	Well, it's about time they knew what they was dealin' with anyway, a coupla lousy no-hopers!
	[*BARNEY's head jerks around and ROO's eyes glint as he sees a weapon for revenge.*]
	Yeah−you, the great lover that's never had a knock back. Tell 'em how lucky you've been lately. Barney [*Almost pleading*] Don't, Roo.

ROO	[*Leaning down to seize him by the lapels*] This is gunna be good! How about the two waitresses at the Greek cafe?
BARNEY	[*Trying to twist aside to escape what is coming*] I never went near them.
ROO	[*Holding him firmly*] You did, they told me. And laughed fit to kill themselves. A fine performance that must have been!
BARNEY	They lied about it.
ROO	[*Dragging him up and shaking him*] Yeah' And I s'pose Mrs Kelly lied when she had you thrown out of the Royal pub? 'N' the cook at Adam's, she was lyin', and the little New Australian woman, and Skinny Linton's missus. All of them lying, and you're still the best there is − like hell you are!
BARNEY	[*Tearing himself free, blazing*] That's enough, Roo.
ROO	[*Towering above him*] And Nancy − after seventeen years, you couldn't even hold Nancy!
BARNEY	You dirty rotten −

[*Angry beyond measure, he seizes the object nearest to his hand. It is the vase containing, among others, the seventeenth doll. This he swings at ROO's head, but the big man rips it from his hands and throws it away into the centre of the room, smashing vase and scattering dolls. OLIVE gives a strangled cry and BUBBA rushes towards her. There is a sudden silence. OLIVE sinks to her knees and picks up the seventeenth doll, holds it close. BUBBA runs up to the windows and exits by the back verandah. The others are unmoving.*]

End of Act 2

Leaving Home

by David French

CAST

(in order of appearance)

    Bill Mercer

    Kathy Jackson

    Jacob Mercer

    Mary Mercer

    Ben Mercer

5 Speaking Parts. No doubling.

The Setting

The scene, which occurs in Act One, Scene One, takes place on a Friday evening in the living and dining rooms of the Mercer's House in Toronto, Canada, in November in the late 1950's. The working-class living room belongs to Newfoundland migrant, Jacob Mercer; a protestant construction worker. A chesterfield sofa, and an armchair are in the living room. In addition a table and chairs are in the dining room. The table is set for 5 and there is a fish meal waiting to be served on the table.

The Extract

The scene takes place on the night of the wedding rehearsal of Bill, aged 17 and Kathy aged 16. When Bill's mother, Mary, answers the door to Kathy she is busy organising the family members to get dressed and eat the meal. Bill is dressed in a tuxedo. Kathy is dressed for a cold Canadian winter's night.

KATHY	Hello, Mrs. Mercer.
MARY	You're just in time, Kathy. [*MARY gives her a kiss.*] Take her coat, Billy. I'll be right out, dear. [*She exits.*]
KATHY	Where is everyone?
BILL	[*Taking her coat*] Getting dressed. [*As he tries to kiss her, she pulls away her cheek.*]
BILL	What's wrong? [*He hangs up her coat.*]
KATHY	Nothing. I don't feel well.
BILL	Why not? Did you drink too much at the party?
KATHY	What party?
BILL	Didn't the girls at work throw a party for you this afternoon?
KATHY	I didn't go to the office this afternoon.
BILL	You didn't go? What do you mean?
KATHY	Just what I said.
BILL	What did you say?
KATHY	Will you get off my back!
BILL	What did I say? [*Slight pause*] Are you mad at me?
KATHY	[*Looks at him.*] Billy, do you love me? Do you? I need to know.
BILL	What's happened, Kathy?
KATHY	I'm asking you a simple question
BILL	And I want to know what's happened.
KATHY	If I hadn't been pregnant, you'd never have wanted to get married, would you?
BILL	So?
KATHY	I hate you.
BILL	For Chrissake, Kathy, what's happened?
KATHY	[*Sits on the chesterfield.*] I lost the baby...
BILL	What?
KATHY	Isn't that good news?
BILL	What the hell happened?
KATHY	I started bleeding in the ladies' room this morning.

BILL	Bleeding? What do you mean?
KATHY	Haemorrhaging. I streamed, and one of the girls rushed me to the hospital. I think the people at work thought I'd done something to myself.
BILL	Had you?
KATHY	Of course not. You know I wouldn't.
BILL	What did the doctor say?
KATHY	I had a miscarriage. [*She looks up at him.*] You're not even sorry, are you?
BILL	I am, really. What did the doctor say?
KATHY	I lost a lot of blood. I'm supposed to eat lots of liver and milk, to build it up. You should have seen me, Billy. I was white and shaky. I'm a little better now. I've been sleeping all afternoon.
BILL	[*Slight pause*] What was it?
KATHY	What was what?
BILL	The baby.
KATHY	Do you really want to know?
	[*BILL doesn't answer.*]
BILL	What'll we do?
KATHY	Tell our folks, I guess. My mother doesn't know yet. She's been at the track all day with her boyfriend, [*Slight pause*] I haven't told anyone else, Billy. Just you.
	[*Enter JACOB and MARY. He is dressed in a pair of slacks and a white shirt. He carries a necktie in his hand. MARY wears a blouse and skirt.*]
JACOB	Billy, my son, tie me a Windsor knot. That's a good boy. [*He hands BILL the necktie and BILL proceeds to make the knot. Shyly, to KATHY*] Hello, my dear. [*KATHY nods.*] Lovely old day.
MARY	Come on. We may as well sit right down before it colds off. I'll serve up the fish and potatoes. [*She transfers the fish and potatoes into serving dishes.*]
JACOB	[*Calling*] Ben! [*To KATHY, referring to the tie*] I'm all t'umbs or I'd do it myself.
BEN	[*Enters, his shirt changed.*] Hi, Kathy.
KATHY	Hi, Ben. Congratulations.

BEN	For what?
KATHY	Didn't you graduate last night?
BEN	Oh. Yeah.
JACOB	I suppose if Ben ever becomes Prime Minister, I'll be the last to know unless I reads it in the newspapers.
MARY	Kathy, you sit right down there, dear. Billy, you sit next to her. And Ben's right here.
	[*BILL hands his father the tie. JACOB slips it on as he approaches the table.*]
	Father, why don't you say grace?
JACOB	Maybe Kathy would like to.
KATHY	We never say grace at our house.
JACOB	Is that a fact? Imagine.
BILL	[*Jumping in*] 'Bless this food that now we take, and feed our souls for Jesus' sake. Amen.'
ALL	Amen. [*They dig in.*]
JACOB	Have an eye to the bones, Kathy. [*Slight pause*] You was born in Toronto, wasn't you? Someday you'll have to take a trip home, you and Billy, and see how they dries the cod on the beaches. He don't remember any more than you. He was just little when he come up here.
MARY	That was a long time ago, Kathy. 1945.
KATHY	[*Slight pause*] Have you been home since, Mr. Mercer?
JACOB	No, my dear, and I don't know if I wants to. A different generation growing up now. [*Glancing at BEN*] A different brand of Newfie altogether. And once the oldtimers die off, that'll be the end of it. Newfoundland'll never be the same after that, I can tell you. [*Slight pause*] Do you know what flakes is?
KATHY	No.
JACOB	Well, they'm spread over the shore – these wooden stages they dries the codfish on. Sometimes – and this is no word of a lie, is it, Mary? – the fishflies'll buzz around that codfish as t'ick as the hairs on your arm. [*Slight pause*] T'icker. T'ick as tarpaper.
MARY	Jacob, we're eating. [*To KATHY*] He's just like his poor mother, Jacob is. She'd start on about the tapeworm as you was lifting the pork to your mouth, [*To JACOB*] Let the poor

girl eat in peace, Father, [*To KATHY*] You've hardly touched your food, dear. Has he spoiled your appetite? It wouldn't be the first time.

KATHY   I'm just not too hungry, Mrs. Mercer.

MARY   I understands. Big day tomorrow. I was the same way, my wedding day. It's a wonder I didn't faint.

JACOB   [*Slight pause – to KATHY*] You notice Ben don't look my way? He's sore.

[*KATHY glances at BEN, who goes on eating, oblivious.*]

JACOB   [*To KATHY*] Oh, he knows how to dish it out with the best, but he can't take it. You can joke with Billy, he likes a bit of fun, but with the other one you don't dare open your mouth.

BEN   Will you shut up, Dad?

JACOB   [*To KATHY*] I'll bet you didn't get sore with your poor father and talk back all the time when he was alive, did you, my dear? No, that's what you didn't. You had more respect. And I bet now you don't regret it.

MARY   Don't ask the child to choose sides, Jacob. You've got no right to do that. Anyhow, Kathy's got more sense than to get mixed up in it. Don't you, Kathy?

JACOB   The Bible says to honour thy father and thy mother....

MARY   [*Exasperated*] Oh, hold your tongue, for goodness sake. Don't your jaw ever get tired?

JACOB   [*To KATHY*] Well, you can see for yourself what happens, my dear. Anyone in this room is free to say what they likes about the old man, but just let him criticize back and you'd t'ink a fox had burst into the chicken coop, the way Mother Mercer here gathers her first-born under her wing. [*Slight pause. To KATHY, but meant for his wife*] I suppose by now you've heard your mother and me once went together? I suppose Minnie's mentioned it often enough? Fine figure of a woman, Minnie. Still looks as good as ever.

BILL   I hear you used to be a real woman's man. Dad.

JACOB   Who told you that?

BILL   Mom.

MARY   [*Quickly*] Liar. I told you no such t'ing.

BILL   You did so. Didn't she, Ben?

[*BEN smiles at his mother.*]

JACOB	Well, contrary to what your mother tells, that particular year I had only one sweetheart, and that was Minnie Jackson. Wasn't it, Mary?
MARY	[*Nodding*] She was still a Fraser then. That was the same year I was going with Jerome McKenzie. Wasn't it, Jacob?
JACOB	Oh, don't forget the most important part, Mary, the Q.C., the Queen's Counsel. Jerome McKenzie, Q.C. [*To KATHY*] Jerome's a well-known barrister in St. John's, and Mrs. Mercer's all the time t'rowing him up in my face. Ain't you, Mary? Never lets me forget it, will you? [*To KATHY*] You see, my dear, she might have married Jerome McKenzie, Q. C., and never had a single worry in the world, if it wasn't for me. Ain't that so, Mary?
MARY	If you insists, Jacob.
	[*BILL and KATHY stare silently at their plates, embarrassed, BEN looks from his father to his mother and then to BILL.*]
BEN	Did you get the boutonnieres and cuff links for the ushers?
MARY	It's all taken care of, my son. [*Pause*] What kind of flowers did your mother order, Kathy?
KATHY	Red roses.
MARY	How nice.
KATHY	I like yellow roses better, but – [*She stops abruptly.*]
BILL	But what?
KATHY	Nothing.
MARY	Yellow roses mean tears, my son.
KATHY	Did you carry roses, Mrs. Mercer?
MARY	I did. Red butterfly roses. And I wore a gown of white satin, with a lace veil. I even had a crown of orange blossoms.
KATHY	I'll bet you were beautiful.
JACOB	My dear, she lit up that little Anglican church like the Second Coming. I suppose I told you all about the wedding ring?
MARY	No, you didn't, and she don't want to hear tell of it, and neither do the rest of us. Don't listen to his big fibs, Kathy.
JACOB	I still remembers that day. I had on my gaberdine suit, with a white carnation in the lapel. In those days Mary t'ought I was handsome.

MARY	Get to the point, Father.
JACOB	We was that poor I couldn't afford a ring, so when the Reverend Mr. Price got t'rough with the dearly beloveds and asked for the ring, I reached into my pocket and give him all I had – an old bent nail.
MARY	Last time it was a cigar band.
JACOB	[*Still to KATHY*] And if you was to ask me today, twenty years later, if it's been worth it – my dear, my answer would still be the same, for all her many faults – that old rusty nail has brung me more joy and happiness than you can ever imagine. And I wouldn't trade the old woman here, nor a blessed hair of her head, not for all the gold bullion in the Vatican.
BILL	Dad.
JACOB	And my name's not Jerome McKenzie, Q.C., either. And the likes of Ben here may t'ink me just an old fool, not worth a second t'ought –
	[*BEN shoves back his plate, holding back his temper.*]
	– and run me down to my face the first chance he gets –
BEN	Ah, shut up.
JACOB	– and treat me with no more respect and consideration than you would your own worst enemy! –
BEN	Will you grow up! [*He knocks over his chair and exits, into his bedroom.*]
JACOB	[*Shouting after him*] – but I've always done what I seen fit, and no man can do more! [*The door slams – slight pause.*] I won't say another word.
MARY	You've said enough, brother. [*Slight pause*] What Kathy must t'ink of us! [*Slight pause*] And then you wonders why he's the way he is, when you sits there brazen-faced and makes him feel like two cents in front of company. You haven't a grain of sense, you haven't!
JACOB	Did I say a word of a lie? Did I?
MARY	No, you always speaks the gospel truth, you do.
JACOB	I never could say two words in a row to that one, without he takes offence. Not two bloody words!
	[*MARY collects the supper plate. BILL and KATHY remain seated.*]

| | Look. He didn't finish half his plate, [*Calling*] Come out and eat the rest of your supper, Ben. There's no food wasted in this house, [*Slight pause*] Take it in to him, Mary. |

MARY   [*Picking up BEN's chair*] You – you're the cause of it. You're enough to spoil anyone's appetite.

JACOB   Ah, for Christ's sake, he's too damn soft, and you don't help any. I was out fishing on the Labrador when I was ten years old, six months of the year for ten dollars, and out of that ten dollars had to come my rubber boots, [*To KATHY*] Ten years old, and I had to stand up and take it like a man. [*To MARY*] That's a lot tougher than a few harsh words from his father!

MARY   [*As she serves the dessert*] And you'll make him hard, is that it, Jacob? Hard and tough like yourself? Blame him for all you've suffered. Make him pay for all you never had.

JACOB   Oh, shut up, Mary, you don't understand these matters. He won't have you or me to fall back on once he gets out into the world. He'll need to be strong or – [*He winks at BILL.*] – he'll end up like your cousin Israel.

MARY   And don't tell that story, Jacob. You're at the table.

JACOB   [*To KATHY*] Israel Parsons was Mrs. Mercer's first cousin.

MARY   Might as well talk to a log.

JACOB   He was a law student at the time, and he worked summers at the pulp and paper mill at Corner Brook, cleaning the machines. Well, one noon hour he crawled inside a machine to clean the big sharp blades, and someone flicked on the switch. Poor young Israel was ground up into pulp. They didn't find a trace of him, did they, Mary? Not even a hair. Mary's poor mother always joked that he was the only one of her relatives ever to make the headlines – if you knows what I mean.

MARY   She knows. And just what has Israel Parsons got to do with Ben, pray tell?

JACOB   Because that's what the world will do to Ben, Mary, if he's not strong. Chew him up alive and swallow him down without a trace. Mark my words. [*He lifts the bowl to his month and drinks the peach juice.*]

An Inspector Calls

by J.B. Priestley

Cast

(in order of appearance)

  Sheila Birling
  Inspector Goole
  Mrs Sybil Birling
  Arthur Birling
  *Eric Birling

4 Speaking parts. No doubling.

*Non-speaking part.

The Setting

The scene, which occurs towards the end of Act Two, takes place in the dining-room of the Birlings' house in Brumley, an industrial city in the North Midlands of England. An evening in Spring, 1912. The dining-room belongs to Arthur Birling, a prosperous manufacturer. The table is laid with a white table cloth there is evidence of the closing stages of a dinner in honour of the engagement of Sheila to Gerald Croft. There is an armchair in the room and a fireplace.

The Extract

Arthur has followed Gerald, to the door of the dining-room and has turned to face his wife. The 'him' Sheila refers to in the dialogue is Gerald. The dinner has been interrupted by the arrival of a Police Inspector who has announced to the family that he is making enquiries concerning the suicide in the town of a young woman. The family is dressed in evening clothes for the dinner and the Inspector wears a day suit.

[*BIRLING crosses up stage to the door to follow him but as he reaches the door the front door slams off stage. MRS BIRLING sits below the table.*]

SHEILA [*To the INSPECTOR*] You know, you never showed him that photograph of her.

INSPECTOR No, it wasn't necessary.

MRS BIRLING You have a photograph of the girl?

INSPECTOR Yes, I think you'd better look at it. [*He comes round right of the table to MRS BIRLING.*]

MRS BIRLING I don't see any particular reason why I should –

INSPECTOR Probably not. But you'd better look at it.

MRS BIRLING Very well.

[*The INSPECTOR produces the photograph and makes MRS BIRLING look hard at it.*]

INSPECTOR [*Taking back the photograph*] You recognise her?

MRS BIRLING No. Why should I?

INSPECTOR Of course she might have changed lately, but I can't believe she could have changed so much.

MRS BIRLING I don't understand you, Inspector.

INSPECTOR [*Moving to the fireplace*] You mean you don't choose to, Mrs Birling.

MRS BIRLING [*Angrily*] I meant what I said.

INSPECTOR You're not telling me the truth.

MRS BIRLING [*Rising*] I beg your pardon!

BIRLING [*Crossing to the table left of MRS BIRLING, angrily lo the INSPECTOR*] Look here, I'm not going to have this, Inspector. You'll apologise at once.

INSPECTOR Apologise for what – doing my duty?

BIRLING No, for being so offensive about it. I'm a public man –

INSPECTOR [*Massively*] Public men, Mr Birling, have responsibilities as well as privileges.

BIRLING Possibly. But you weren't asked to come here to talk to me about my responsibilities.

SHEILA Let's hope not. Though I'm beginning to wonder.

MRS BIRLING Does that mean anything, Sheila?

SHEILA [*Rising*] It means that we've no excuses now for putting on airs and that if we've any sense we won't try. Father threw this girl out because she asked for decent wages. I went and pushed her further out, right into the street, just because I was angry and she was pretty. Gerald set her up as his mistress and then dropped her when it suited him. And now you're pretending you don't recognise her from that photograph. I admit I don't know why you should, but I know jolly well you did in fact recognise her, from the way you looked. And if you're not telling the truth, why should the Inspector apologise? And can't you see, both of you, you're making it worse?

[*We hear the front door slam.*]

BIRLING That was the door again.

MRS BIRLING Gerald must have come back.

INSPECTOR Unless your son has just gone out.

BIRLING I'll see.

[*He turns to the door and goes out quickly. The INSPECTOR turns to MRS BIRLING.*]

INSPECTOR Mrs Birling, you're a member – a prominent member – of the Brumley Women's Charity Organisation, aren't you?

[*MRS BIRLING sits below the table. She does not reply.*]

SHEILA Go on, Mother. You might as well admit it. [*To the INSPECTOR*] Yes, she is. Why? [*She sits left of the table.*]

INSPECTOR [*Crossing down stage to the desk; calmly*] It's an organisation to which women in distress can appeal for help in various forms. Isn't that so?

MRS BIRLING [*With dignity*] Yes. We've done a great deal of useful work in helping deserving cases.

INSPECTOR There was a meeting of the interviewing committee two weeks ago?

MRS BIRLING I dare say there was.

INSPECTOR You know very well there was, Mrs Birling. You were in the chair.

MRS BIRLING And if I was, what business is it of yours?

INSPECTOR [*Severely*] Do you want me to tell you – in plain words?

[*BIRLING enters. He is looking rather agitated. He closes the door.*]

BIRLING	That must have been Eric.
MRS BIRLING	[*Alarmed*] Have you been up to his room?
BIRLING	Yes. And I called out on both landings. It must have been Eric we heard go out then.
MRS BIRLING	Silly boy! Where can he have gone to?
BIRLING	I can't imagine. But he was in one of his excitable queer moods, and even though we don't need him here –
INSPECTOR	[*Cutting in, sharply*] We do need him here. And if he's not back soon, I shall have to go and find him.

[*BIRLING and MRS BIRLING exchange bewildered and rather frightened glances.*]

SHEILA	[*Rising and crossing above the table to the fireplace*] He's probably just gone to cool off. He'll be back soon.
INSPECTOR	[*Severely*] I hope so.
MRS BIRLING	And why should you hope so?
INSPECTOR	[*Crossing to left of MRS BIRLING*] I'll explain why when you've answered my questions, Mrs Birling.
BIRLING	Is there any reason why my wife should answer questions from you, Inspector?
INSPECTOR	Yes, a very good reason. You'll remember that Mr Croft told us - quite truthfully, I believe - that he hadn't spoken to or seen Eva Smith since last September. But Mrs Birling spoke to and saw her only two weeks ago.
SHEILA	[*Astonished*] Mother!
BIRLING	Is this true?
MRS BIRLING	[*After a pause*] Yes, quite true.

[*SHEILA sits in the armchair.*]

INSPECTOR	She appealed to your organisation for help?
MRS BIRLING	Yes.
INSPECTOR	Not as Eva Smith?
MRS BIRLING	No. Nor as Daisy Renton.
INSPECTOR	As what then?
MRS BIRLING	First, she called herself Mrs Birling –
BIRLING	[*Astounded*] Mrs Birling!

MRS BIRLING   Yes. I think it was simply a piece of gross impertinence – quite deliberate – and naturally that was one of the things that prejudiced me against her case.

BIRLING   [*Crossing up to the sideboard*] And I should think so! Damned impudence! [*He pours himself a drink.*]

INSPECTOR   You admit being prejudiced against her case?

MRS BIRLING   Yes.

SHEILA   Mother, she's just died a horrible death – don't forget.

[*The INSPECTOR moves up left, above the chair left of the table.*]

MRS BIRLING   I'm very sorry. But I think she had only herself to blame.

INSPECTOR   Was it owing to your influence, as the most prominent member of the Committee, that help was refused the girl?

MRS BIRLING   Possibly.

INSPECTOR   Was it or was it not your influence?

[*BIRLING moves down to the fireplace.*]

MRS BIRLING   [*Rising and moving away to right; stung*] Yes, it was. I didn't like her manner. She'd impertinently made use of our name, though she pretended afterwards it just happened to be the first she thought of. She had to admit, after I began questioning her, that she had no claim to the name, that she wasn't married, and that the story she told at first – about a husband who'd deserted her – was quite false. It didn't take me long to get the truth – or some of the truth – out of her.

INSPECTOR   Why did she ask for help?

MRS BIRLING   [*Moving up to the right end of the sideboard*] You know very well why she asked for help.

INSPECTOR   No, I don't. I know why she needed help. But as I wasn't there, I don't know what she asked it for from your committee.

MRS BIRLING   I don't think we need discuss it.

INSPECTOR   You have no hope of not discussing it, Mrs Birling.

MRS BIRLING   [*Turning on the INSPECTOR*] If you think you can bring any pressure to bear upon me, Inspector, you're quite mistaken. Unlike the other three, I did nothing I'm ashamed of or that won't bear investigation. The girl asked for assistance. We are asked to look carefully into the claims made upon us. I wasn't satisfied with this girl's claim – she seemed to me to be not a good case – and so I used my influence to have it refused. And in spite of what's happened to the girl since, I consider I did my duty. [*As she moves to the fireplace up stage of Mr BIRLING.*] So if I prefer not to discuss it any further, you have no power to make me change my mind.

INSPECTOR   Yes I have.

MRS BIRLING   [*Turning to face the INSPECTOR*] No you haven't. Simply because I've done nothing wrong – and you know it.

INSPECTOR   [*Very deliberately*] I think you did something terribly wrong – and that you're going to spend the rest of your life regret ling it. I wish you'd been with me tonight in the Infirmary. You'd have seen –

SHEILA   [*Bursting in*] No, no, please! Not that again. I've imagined it enough already.

INSPECTOR   [*Very deliberately*] Then the next time you imagine it, just remember that this girl was going to have a child.

SHEILA   [*Horrified*] No! Oh – horrible – horrible! How could she have wanted to kill herself.

INSPECTOR   Because she'd been turned out and turned down too many times. This was the end.

SHEILA   Mother, you must have known.

INSPECTOR   It was because she was going to have a child that she went for assistance to your mother's committee.

BIRLING   Look here, this wasn't Gerald Croft –

INSPECTOR   [*Cutting in, sharply*] No, no. Nothing to do with him.

SHEILA   Thank goodness for that! Though I don't know why I should care now.

INSPECTOR   [*To MRS BIRLING*] And you've nothing further to tell me, eh?

MRS BIRLING   I'll tell you what I told her. Go and look for the father of the child. It's his responsibility.

INSPECTOR   That doesn't make it any the less yours. She came to you for help, at a time when no woman could have needed it more. And you not only refused it yourself but saw to it that the others refused it too. She was here alone, almost penniless, desperate. She needed not only money but advice, sympathy, friendliness. You've had children. You must have known what she was feeling. And you slammed the door in her face.

SHEILA   [*With feeling*] Mother, I think it was cruel and vile.

BIRLING   [*Dubiously*] I must say, Sybil, that when this comes out at the inquest, it isn't going to do us much good. The Press might easily take it up −

MRS BIRLING [*Agitated now*] Oh, stop it, both of you. And please remember before you start accusing me of anything again that it wasn't I who had her turned out of her employment-which probably began it all. [*She turns to the INSPECTOR, moves to the chair below the table and sits.*]

[*BIRLING sits in the chair from right of the table.*]

In the circumstances I think I was justified. The girl had begun by telling us a pack of lies. Afterwards, when I got at the truth, I discovered that she knew who the father was, she was quite certain about that, and so I told her it was her business to make him responsible. If he refused to marry her − and in my opinion he ought to be compelled to − then he must at least support her.

INSPECTOR   And what did she reply to that?

MRS BIRLING [*Rising and crossing down left*] Oh-a lot of silly nonsense.

INSPECTOR   What was it?

MRS BIRLING [*Moving to the desk*] Whatever it was, I know it made me finally lose all patience with her. She was giving herself ridiculous airs. She was claiming elaborate fine feelings and scruples that were simply absurd in a girl in her position.

INSPECTOR   [*Very sternly*] Her position now is that she lies with a burnt-out inside on a slab.

[*BIRLING rises and tries to protest.*]

[*He turns on BIRLING.*] Don't stammer and yammer at me again, man. I'm losing all patience with you people. What did she say?

MRS BIRLING [*Rather cowed*] She said that the father was only a youngster − silly and wild and drinking too much. There couldn't be any question of marrying him − it would be wrong for them both. He had given her money but she didn't want to take any more money from him.

INSPECTOR   Why didn't she want to take any more money from him?

MRS BIRLING [*Crossing to the fireplace*] All a lot of nonsense – I didn't believe a word of it.

INSPECTOR I'm not asking you if you believed it. I want to know what she said.

Why didn't she want to take any more money from this boy?

MRS BIRLING. Oh – she had some fancy reason. As if a girl of that sort would ever refuse money!

INSPECTOR [*Moving behind the table towards MRS BIRLING; sternly*] I warn you, you're making it worse for yourself. What reason did she give for not taking any more money?

MRS BIRLING Her story was – that he'd said something one night, when he was drunk, that gave her the idea that it wasn't his money.

INSPECTOR Where had he got it from then?

MRS BIRLING He'd stolen it.

INSPECTOR [*Turning and moving slowly left*] So she'd come to you for assistance because she didn't want to take stolen money?

MRS BIRLING That's the story she finally told, after I'd refused to believe her original story – that she was a married woman who'd been deserted by her husband. I didn't see any reason to believe that one story should be any truer than the other. Therefore, you're quite wrong to suppose I shall regret what I did.

[*She sits behind the table.*]

INSPECTOR [*Turning to MRS BIRLING*] But if her story was true, if this boy had been giving her stolen money, then she came to you for help because she wanted to keep this youngster out of any more trouble – isn't that so?

MRS BIRLING Possibly. But it sounded ridiculous to me. So I was perfectly justified in advising my committee not to allow her claim for assistance.

INSPECTOR You're not even sorry now, when you know what happened to the girl?

MRS BIRLING I'm sorry she should have come to such a horrible end. But I accept no blame for it at all.

INSPECTOR Who is to blame then?

MRS BIRLING First the girl herself.

SHEILA   [*Bitterly*] For letting father and me have her chucked out of her jobs?

MRS BIRLING   Secondly, I blame the young man who was the father of the child she was going to have. If, as she said, he didn't belong to her class, and was some drunken young idler, then that's all the more reason why he shouldn't escape. He should be made an example of. If the girl's death is due to anybody, then it's due to him.

INSPECTOR   And if her story is true – that he was stealing money –

MRS BIRLING   [*Rather agitated now*] There's no point in assuming that –

INSPECTOR   But supposing we do, what then?

MRS BIRLING   Then he'd be entirely responsible – because the girl wouldn't have come to us, and have been refused assistance, if it hadn't been for him –

INSPECTOR   So he's the chief culprit anyhow?

MRS BIRLING   Certainly. And he ought to be dealt with very severely –

SHEILA   [*Rising and crossing to MRS BIRLING with sudden alarm*] Mother – stop – stop.

BIRLING   Be quiet, Sheila!

SHEILA   But don't you see –

MRS BIRLING   [*Severely*] You're behaving like a hysterical child tonight.

[*SHEILA moves up right of the table.*]

MRS BIRLING   [*She turns to the INSPECTOR.*] And if you'd take some steps to find this young man and then make sure that he's compelled to confess in public his responsibility – instead of staying here asking quite unnecessary questions – then you really would be doing your duty.

INSPECTOR   [*Grimly*] Don't worry, Mrs Birling. I shall do my duty! [*He looks at his watch.*]

MRS BIRLING   [*Triumphantly*] I'm glad to hear it.

INSPECTOR   No hushing up, eh? Make an example of the young man; eh? Public confession of responsibility – um?

MRS BIRLING   Certainly. I consider it your duty. [*She rises.*] And now no doubt you'd like to say good-night.

INSPECTOR   Not yet. I'm waiting. [*He moves to the chair left of the table and sits.*]

MRS BIRLING   Waiting for what?

BIRLING   [*Terrified now*] Look, Inspector, you're not trying to tell us that my boy – is mixed up in this –?

INSPECTOR   [*Sternly*] If he is, then we know what to do, don't we? Mrs Birling has just told us.

BIRLING   [*Crossing to MRS BIRLING, thunderstruck*] My God! By – look here –

MRS BIRLING [*Agitatedly*] I don't believe it. I won't believe it... [*She sits below the table.*]

SHEILA   [*Moving behind MRS BIRLING and kneeling*] Mother – I begged and begged you to stop –

[*The INSPECTOR holds up a hand. We hear the front door. The INSPECTOR rises and turns to face the door. They all wait, looking towards the door. ERIC enters, looking extremely pale and distressed. He meets their enquiring stares. There is a little cry from MRS BIRLING as –*

the curtain falls quickly.]

Top Girls

by Caryl Churchill

Cast

(in order of appearance)

    Marlene

    Angie

    Mrs Kidd

3 Speaking parts. No doubling.

The Setting

The scene, which occurs in Act Two, Scene Three, takes place in London, U.K., in the main office of the 'Top Girls' employment agency where Marlene works. The scene, which is set in the early 1980's, takes place in the morning. There is a desk with a phone on it and two chairs.

The Scene

Career woman, Marlene, is in the main office when her niece, Angie, from 'up north' unexpectedly arrives in the office. Angie suspects that Marlene is in fact her mother.

[*Main office.*

MARLENE and ANGIE. ANGIE arrive.]

ANGIE	Hello.
MARLENE	Have you an appointment?
ANGIE	It's me. I've come.
MARLENE	What? It's not Angie?
ANGIE	It was hard to find this place. I got lost.
MARLENE	How did you get past the receptionist? The girl on the desk, didn't she try to stop you?
ANGIE	What desk?
MARLENE	Never mind.
ANGIE	I just walked in. I was looking for you.
MARLENE	Well you found me.
ANGIE	Yes.
MARLENE	So where's your mum? Are you up in town for the day?
ANGIE	Not really.
MARLENE	Sit down. Do you feel all right?
ANGIE	Yes thank you.
MARLENE	So where's Joyce?
ANGIE	She's at home.
MARLENE	Did you come up on a school trip then?
ANGIE	I've left school.
MARLENE	Did you come up with a friend?
ANGIE	No. There's just me.
MARLENE	You came up by yourself, that's fun. What have you been doing? Shopping? Tower of London?
ANGIE	No, I just come here. I come to you.
MARLENE	That's very nice of you to think of paying your aunty a visit. There's not many nieces make that the first port of call. Would you like a cup of coffee?
ANGIE	No thank you.
MARLENE	Tea, orange?
ANGIE	No thank you.

MARLENE	Do you feel all right?
ANGIE	Yes thank you.
MARLENE	Are you tired from the journey?
ANGIE	Yes, I'm tired from the journey.
MARLENE	You sit there for a bit then. How's Joyce?
ANGIE	She's all right.
MARLENE	Same as ever.
ANGIE	Oh yes.
MARLENE	Unfortunately you've picked a day when I'm rather busy, if there's ever a day when I'm not, or I'd take you out to lunch and we'd go to Madame Tussaud's. We could go shopping. What time do you have to be back? Have you got a day return?
ANGIE	No.
MARLENE	So what train are you going back on?
ANGIE	I came on the bus.
MARLENE	So what bus are you going back on? Are you staying the night?
ANGIE	Yes.
MARLENE	Who are you staying with? Do you want me to put you up for the night, is that it?
ANGIE	Yes please.
MARLENE	I haven't got a spare bed.
ANGIE	I can sleep on the floor.
MARLENE	You can sleep on the sofa.
ANGIE	Yes please.
MARLENE	I do think Joyce might have phoned me. It's like her.
ANGIE	This is where you work is it?
MARLENE	It's where I have been working the last two years but I'm going to move into another office.
ANGIE	It's lovely.
MARLENE	My new office is nicer than this. There's just the one big desk in it for me.
ANGIE	Can I see it?

MARLENE	Not now, no, there's someone else in it now. But he's leaving at the end of next week and I'm going to do his job.
ANGIE	Is that good?
MARLENE	Yes, it's very good.
ANGIE	Are you going to be in charge?
MARLENE	Yes I am.
ANGIE	I knew you would be.
MARLENE	How did you know?
ANGIE	I knew you'd be in charge of everything.
MARLENE	Not quite everything.
ANGIE	You will be.
MARLENE	Well we'll see.
ANGIE	Can I see it next week then?
MARLENE	Will you still be here next week?
ANGIE	Yes.
MARLENE	Don't you have to go home?
ANGIE	No.
MARLENE	Why not?
ANGIE	It's all right.
MARLENE	Is it all right?
ANGIE	Yes, don't worry about it.
MARLENE	Does Joyce know where you are?
ANGIE	Yes of course she does.
MARLENE	Well does she?
ANGIE	Don't worry about it.
MARLENE	How long are you planning to stay with me then?
ANGIE	You know when you came to see us last year?
MARLENE.	Yes, that was nice wasn't it?
ANGIE	That was the best day of my whole life.
MARLENE	So how long are you planning to stay?
ANGIE	Don't you want me?
MARLENE	Yes, yes, I just wondered.

ANGIE	I won't stay if you don't want me.
MARLENE	No, of course you can stay.
ANGIE	I'll sleep on the floor. I won't be any bother.
MARLENE	Don't get upset.
ANGIE	I'm not, I'm not. Don't worry about it.
	[*MRS KIDD comes in.*]
MRS KIDD	Excuse me.
MARLENE	Yes.
MRS KIDD	Excuse me.
MARLENE	Can I help you?
MRS KIDD	Excuse me bursting in on you like this but I have to talk to you.
MARLENE	I am engaged at the moment. / If you could go to reception –
MRS KIDD	I'm Rosemary Kidd, Howard's wife, you don't recognise me but we did meet, I remember you of course but / you wouldn't –
MARLENE	Yes of course, Mrs Kidd, I'm sorry, we did meet. Howard's about somewhere I expect, have you looked in his office?
MRS KIDD	Howard's not about, no. I'm afraid it's you I've come to see if I could have a minute or two.
MARLENE	I do have an appointment in five minutes.
MRS KIDD	This won't take five minutes. I'm very sorry. It is a matter of some urgency.
MARLENE	Well of course. What can I do for you?
MRS KIDD	I just wanted a chat, an informal chat. It's not something I can simply – I'm sorry if I'm interrupting your work. I know office work isn't like housework / which is all interruptions.
MARLENE	No, no, this is my niece. Angie. Mrs Kidd.
MRS KIDD	Very pleased to meet you.
ANGIE	Very well thank you.
MRS KIDD	Howard's not in today.
MARLENE	Isn't he?
MRS KIDD	He's feeling poorly.
MARLENE	I didn't know. I'm sorry to hear that.

MRS KIDD   The fact is he's in a state of shock. About what's happened.

MARLENE.   What has happened?

MRS KIDD   You should know if anyone. I'm referring to you being appointed managing director instead of Howard. He hasn't been at all well all weekend. He hasn't slept for three nights. I haven't slept.

MARLENE   I'm sorry to hear that, Mrs Kidd. Has he thought of taking sleeping pills?

MRS KIDD   It's very hard when someone has worked all these years.

MARLENE   Business life is full of little setbacks. I'm sure Howard knows that. He'll bounce back in a day or two. We all bounce back.

MRS KIDD   If you could see him you'd know what I'm talking about. What's it going to do to him working for a woman? I think if it was a man he'd get over it as something normal.

MARLENE   I think he's going to have to get over it.

MRS KIDD   It's me that bears the brunt. I'm not the one that's been promoted. I put him first every inch of the way. And now what do I get? You women this, you women that. It's not my fault. You're going to have to be very careful how you handle him. He's very hurt.

MARLENE   Naturally I'll be tactful and pleasant to him, you don't start pushing someone round. I'll consult him over any decisions affecting his department. But that's no different, Mrs Kidd, from any of my other colleagues.

MRS KIDD   I think it is different, because he's a man.

MARLENE   I'm not quite sure why you came to see me.

MRS KIDD   I had to do something.

MARLENE   Well you've done it, you've seen me. I think that's probably all we've time for. I'm sorry he's been taking it out on you. He really is a shit, Howard.

MRS KIDD   But he's got a family to support. He's got three children. It's only fair.

MARLENE   Are you suggesting I give up the job to him then?

MRS KIDD   It had crossed my mind if you were unavailable after all for some reason, he would be the natural second choice I think, don't you? I'm not asking.

MARLENE   Good.

MRS KIDD	You mustn't tell him I came. He's very proud.
MARLENE	If he doesn't like what's happening here he can go and work somewhere else.
MRS KIDD	Is that a threat?
MARLENE	I'm sorry but I do have some work to do.
MRS KIDD	It's not that easy, a man of Howard's age. You don't care. I thought he was going too far but he's right. You're one of these ballbreakers / that's what you are. You'll end up...
MARLENE	I'm sorry but I do have some work to do.
MRS KIDD	Miserable and lonely. You're not natural.
MARLENE	Could you please piss off?
MRS KIDD	I thought if I saw you at least I'd be doing something.
	[*MRS KIDD goes.*]
MARLENE	I've got to go and do some work now. Will you come back later?
ANGIE	I think you were wonderful.
MARLENE	I've got to go and do some work now.
ANGIE	You told her to piss off.
MARLENE	Will you come back later?
ANGIE	Can't I stay here?
MARLENE	Don't you want to go sightseeing?
ANGIE	I'd rather stay here.
MARLENE	You can stay here I suppose, if it's not boring.
ANGIE	It's where I most want to be in the world.
MARLENE	I'll see you later then.
	[*MARLENE goes.*]
	[*ANGIE sits at WIN's desk.*]

Rudali

By Usha Ganguli

Translated by Anjum Katyal

Cast

(In order of appearance)

    Bikhni

    Sanichari

    Misri [a woman neighbour]

    Dulan's Wife

    Bijua [the village barber]

    Dulan

6 Speaking parts. No doubling.

Setting

The scene, which occurs towards the end of the play in Scenes 6 and 7, takes place in Sanichari's modest home of in Tahad Village, Bengal, India on an evening in the late 1980's. The home belongs to a low-caste Indian widow, Sanichari. She shares her home with another woman called Bikhni.

The Extract

Sanichari, an honest, simple woman, has been forced to live on her own resources and has only one person in the world to live for, her grandson. She is returning from the mela [market] when she meets by accident a friend from her younger days called Bikhni. She is also a widow and has lost her family because of falling out over bad debts resulting from her son's wedding. She has a small amount of money and has joined forces with Sanichari in terms of surviving and earning a living by any means possible.

Scene 6

[*Evening. SANICHARI's home. The house is looking neat
and cared for, with a freshly washed covering on the
charpoy. BIKHNI, seated on a low stool, is humming to
herself as she carefully oils, combs and plaits SANICHARI's
hair.*]

BIKHNI   *Arre* you wretch, what a state your hair is in! Crawling with
lice – whole fields of them!

SANICHARI   Nibbling away at me all day… and because of these damned
lice even my nights were ruined – I couldn't sleep!

BIKHNI   You were messy even as a child. Those huge, long nails, oily,
uncombed hair!

SANICHARI   And what about your black ghagra! Ram, Ram! It stank so
much even dogs were scared away!

BIKHNI   Hold still, you black-tongued woman! Let me massage the
oil in properly! Here, pass me the comb.

SANICHARI   Look beside you, it must be there. [*BIKHNI gets up and
fetches the comb.*] We've used up so much oil. Bikhni!

BIKHNI   Shh, sit still...

SANICHARI   Where did I ever get the time to do my hair or dress up,
Bikhni? My life has been nothing but the stove, the chakki,
and outside jobs. If you had been in the same situation you
would have realized...

BIKHNI   Oh I, of course, was lording it like a queen, feasting on
sweetmeats all day! *Arre*, what can you do, such is a
woman's lot...

SANICHARI   If my bahu had been half-way decent, I would have been
better off. As it is, I divided my time between cleaning up
my in-laws' shit and piss, and tending to my Budhua. My
son died, my daughter-in-law ran off… I brought up my
grandson, looked after him till he was a young man, and
then he went off with the no-good magicians… My whole life
has been spent working, working....

BIKHNI   What a life! Full of tears, sorrow...

SANICHARI   No, I never had the time to weep. They all died, one by one.
My in-laws, my brother-in-law and his wife, my husband,
my son. I didn't shed a single tear. They call me a *daain* –
say it's as if I was born just to devour others.

BIKHNI	Which son of a bitch dares call you a daain'? I'll scratch his eyes out! Don't worry, Sanichari, you'll see everything will turn out fine. I'll get hold of some fertilizer from the government office and start growing vegetables once again, and I'll sell them myself in the market.
	[*BIKHNI completes plaiting SANICHARI's hair, and takes a look at her handiwork. Something strikes her. She fetches something from her bundle.*]
SANICHARI	What's happened?
BIKHNI	Wait a minute.
SANICHARI	What's this ...?
BIKHNI	Wait a bit ... [*She puts a pair of earrings on SANICHARI*] let me put them on. I had bought them at the mela for myself. Just see how nice they look!
SANICHARI	Go on with you!
BIKHNI	Stop acting coy! [*She gets up and fetches the mirror.*] Go ahead, take a good look. [*Sanichari casts a quick glance at herself, then, embarrassed, puts the mirror away.*]
SANICHARI	This is the first time in my whole life that anyone has given me a gift...no, no, once my husband also... he took me to the Baisakhi mela at Tohri. He bought me lots of red and yellow bangles, and some alta, but...
BIKHNI	What happened?
SANICHARI	The next day I threw everything into the river, the bangles, the alta, my sindoor...
BIKHNI	Why?
SANICHARI	He paid a rupee and bought some of the milk that had been blessed by Sliivji Maharnj. The milk was stale, it had gone sour...within three hours he got severe cholera and died right there, in the government hospital...
BIKHNI	My god! Cholera from sacred offerings?
SANICHARI	What else d'you expect from a poor man's god? D'you know, because I was alone, I was forced to perform two kriya ceremonies for my dead husband?
BIKHNI	Really?
SANICHARI	Really. The Tohri panda told me that since you're here, you must make the pinda offering before you go. I paid a rupee and a quarter for an offering of sand and sattu. What a to-do there was in our village panchayat over this! That bastard

Mohanlal said, how can a Tohri brahman know how we hold a kriya ceremony in Tahad village! He landed me with a second kriya ceremony. I had to feed the whole village on curds and chivda after taking a loan from Ramavatar.

BIKHNI   D'you mean to say that the brahmans of Tohri village are different from the brahmans of Tahad villager?

SANICHARI Who knows... the thakurs and brahmans are all in this together. They control everything. It took me five years to pay off my debt to the thakur.

BIKHNI   All these bastards are the same! [*They clean the dishes, put them away, and drink some water.*] Come, let's get some sleep.

SANICHARI You haven't sat still a moment since you've come! You cleaned out the house, made cowdung cakes, picked the lice out of my hair, you want to plant the vegetable patch tomorrow morning – I'm telling you, Bikhni, in my whole life nobody has ever done so much for me. No one has even thought of me as a human being!

BIKHNI   Why are you keeping a tally? Whatever I've done is for us, after all – not for someone else. Go to sleep now.

SANICHARI You know, when I was a girl my mother used to always tell me that a woman's worst enemy was other women...

BIKHNI   *Arre*, that's all stuff made up by men. Go on, go to sleep.

SANICHARI Tonight I'll sleep peacefully...

[*They lie dawn beside each other and fall asleep. The light dims slowly.*]

Scene 7

[*Morning. SANICHARI's home. SANICHARI and BIKHNI are squatting and counting their money. A pot lies beside them. SANICHARI turns it upside down, and BIKHNI starts to sort out the money. The counting begins.*]

SANICHARI Twenty plus twenty makes forty, plus five makes forty-five and thirty and seventy-five paise –

BIKHNI   Not thirty, forty.

SANICHARI How forty? Now look what you've done, you've mixed me up again.

BIKHNI   I've mixed you up? You've been counting all wrong from the start!

SANICHARI Okay, wait, let me start again. Look, here's fifty paise, here's forty, that makes eighty –

BIKHNI *Arre*, idiot, do forty and fifty make eighty?

SANICHARI Yes – no, no, wait a bit [*Counts on her fingers*] sixty, seventy, eighty, ninety – okay, ninety and thirty... that makes one rupee twenty paise, doesn't it?

BlKHNI Yes...

SANICHARI Five and five ten, plus five fifteen, and... [*Misri enters.*]

MISRI So then, Sanichari, what's happening? [*Sanichari's calculations get disturbed again.*]

SANICHARI Oh, we're busy making sweetmeats for your wedding, that's all – come, join us!

MISRI Why are you so bad tempered? I just came to get news of your friend here. [*To Kikhni*] How are you, sister?

SANICHARI Got your news? Now you can leave. Misri heard that your friend brought a whole lot of money with her ...

BIKHNI Yes... a whole treasure-chest full! Can't you see? No matter how much we count, there's still more . . .

MISRI Having fun, eh, Sanichari?

SANICHARI Oh, yes, loads of fun. Tell you what, Misri – leave your husband and come live here with us. Then all three of us can have lots of fun...

MISRI Why are you talking rubbish, Sanichari! You have a filthy mind! I just come here to ask after your friend, and you start insulting me!

SANICHARI Run along, now. All morning she's been hovering around us! [*MISRI leaves.*] She's an out-and-out bitch, that old hag! She's mixed me up completely... fifty and forty makes –

BIKHNI That's enough, stop, you've done enough counting! [*She counts.*] Altogether it comes to two rupees and thirty paise!

SANICHARI *Hai Maiyya!* Just two rupees thirty paise! That's all that's left!

BIKHNI What do you expect? D'you think we can live a lifetime on thirty rupees?

SANICHARI Now what will happen?

BIKHNI We're in trouble... there aren't any vegetables in the yard either.

SANICHARI We used up all your money, Bikhni...

BIKHNI What's this 'your' money business? The money was there, it got used up, that's all there is to it.

[*SANICHARI keeps quiet.*] You still haven't accepted me as your own, Sanichari.

[*DULAN's voice is heard, off, raised in anger.*]

DULAN'S WIFE *Hai*, may you die, you bastards! May you perish in flames! If I catch you, I'll roast you in the oven! *Arre*, why are you running away, you brats, if you have the guts come and face me! Come on!

BIKHNI Sounds like Lachmi.

SANICHARI [*Peering out*] What's happened, O Mother of Dhatua?

DULAN'S WIFE [*As she enters*]. Damn brats!

SANICHARI Why were you screaming like that? Aren't you going to tell us?

DULAN'S WIFE Should I sit quietly and let those bastards get away with it? The next time they enter my courtyard I'll break their legs!

SANICHARI *Arre*, will you tell us what happened, or are you going to keep blathering on like this?

DULAN'S WIFE I spent hours carefully grinding the dal to make *badis* and put them out into the sun to harden, and those bastards came and stole them all!

SANICHARI Who? Who stole them?

DULAN'S WIFE Hanumanji's descendants, those damned monkeys!

BIKHNI Monkeys...? You mean all this time you've been carrying on about monkeys! [*She laughs.*]

DULAN'S WIFE What're you grinning about? If that marauding army of bastards had laid your vegetable patch to waste you would know how it feels...

DULAN [*Entering*] *Arre*, why are you cursing Ramji's disciples so roundly?

DULAN'S WIFE Now don't you start! All my hard work.

SANICHARI [*Arranging the charpoy*] All right, now calm down.

BIKHNI We'll make you some more badis.

SANICHARI	Come, sit down, Dulan. It's good that you're here. Only you can help us.
DULAN	Now what's the matter?
SANICHARI	What can I say? All our savings are gone. There are no vegetables to sell. From tomorrow we'll have to starve.
DULAN	Why should you starve when there are so many ways of earning a living?
BIKHNI	It's the malik-mahajans who have ways of earning open to them. Us dushads and ganjus have to make our own openings.
DULAN	So go ahead and make them. Across the river there's a road being built for the Devi's temple. Dhatua was telling me that they're looking for labourers. Go there with your friend and set to work.
DULAN'S WIFE	In your dotage you re losing whatever little brains you had! You expect them to break stones at their age!
DULAN	*Arre*, if they can't break stones, they can pick one up, can't they?
SANICHARI	What do you mean?
DULAN	Early in the morning, when there's no one about, when everyone's sleeping, quietly make your way to the river and pick up a black stone from the riverbank.
SANICHARI	A black stone?
DULAN	Let me finish. Then you wash and bathe that stone, anoint it with oil, put sindoor on it and take your place in the Tohri market place.
SANICHARI	Then?
DULAN	Then? Then you announce to everyone that Mahavirji visited you in your dreams and granted you a vision. Wait and see how the devout will throng to make offerings to your stone!
BIKHNI	This is a fine opening you've shown us, Dulan! We'll rake in the money!
SANICHARI	Quiet! Making mockery of the gods! All my life I've worked hard to earn my living – and now, in my old age, am I to fool around like this with something sacred?
DULAN	Well, you can consider it fooling around, or mockery, if you wish. But it just shows that you have a wicked mind. That's why you see something sinful wherever you look.

SANICHARI How come?

DULAN How come? I'll tell you. Now, you know Lachman's old mother has joint pains, don't you?

SANICHARI Yes, she does.

DULAN That old woman handed me ten rupees and said – Dulan Bhaiya, fetch me some of Deviji's oil from the market, won't you? I said okay, but who's going to go haring off to the market just for that old hag? Two days later I took some oil from home and handed it to her. She applied that oil and a couple of days later that same bedridden old creature was hopping gaily all over the village on her own two legs...

BIKHNI You save your tallest tales for us old women, huh, Dulan?

DULAN I swear on Ram Bhagwan that every word is god's own truth. *Arre*, if your mind is pure then your actions are pure! I'm telling you, Sanichari, no god is more important than your belly. One does whatever it takes to feed one's stomach. [*An agitated Bijua enters.*]

BIJUA Dulan Bhaiya, *arre* O Dulan Bhaiya!

DULAN What's the matter? What's happened?

BIJUA *Arre*, there's a big to-do in the village! Bhairo Singh of Barohi village has been murdered!

WOMEN [*Together*]. Hai Ram!

DULAN What're you saying...?

BIJUA Yes, Bhaiya. This morning at daybreak Bhairo Singh's corpse was found lying in the middle of the fields.

DULAN What...?

BIJUA And the murderer is his son Madho Singh,

DULAN Really?

BIJUA That's what the villagers all say.

SANICHARI Hai Maiyya!

BIKHNI What a world this is – a son killing his father!

BIJUA. The world of the wealthy is different from ours. For the sake of money, a mother can kill her son, a son his mother.

DULAN Achha, has Madho Singh been caught yet?

BIJUA Are you crazy? Will the police arrest someone like him? These people have the power of money – the law, the police, the government, are all firmly in their grasp.

SANICHARI Bhairo Singh may have died, but your luck has blossomed...

BIJUA. Why not! Just wait and see what a fancy kriya ceremony Madho Singh will arrange for his father!

Already two and a half maunds of sandalwood, pure ghee and incense have been sent for. Know what, Dulan Bhaiya, he's even sent for whores to wail at the funeral!

DULAN Really?

BIJUA Okay, I'm off. I still have to inform Mohanial – I thought I'd stop off on the way and tell you people first. Okay, I'm going now, Bhaiya [*Leaves hastily*]

SANICHARI *Arre* Bijua, at least have a glass of water –

BIJUA [*Over his shoulder*] No, no, Bhauji, some other time.

DULAN How about it, Sanichari?

SANICHARI What...?

DULAN Arre, a thakur has died, mourners are bound to be required. Do one thing, the two of you present yourselves–

BIKHNI Are there no family members to weep for him?

DULAN Only the families of the poor mourn their dead. The rich households have to hire mourners. Arre, if you mourn for them you'll get money, grain, and the day after the kriya you'll even get clothes and a good meal.

SANICHARI *Hai Maiyya*, are you suggesting that I should mourn? Me? I haven't been able to shed a tear, ever. When Budhua's father died, I thought at least then I would really cry hard. I even went and sat under a peepul tree and all day I kept thinking now I'll cry, now I'll cry – then it became evening and I hadn't shed a single tear.

DULAN Arre, that's not the kind of crying I'm talking of. This is crying for money, crying as a business. Just do it the way you would grind wheat or carry bricks for the sake of a daily wage.

BIKHNI Take me to them, Dulan, I can cry magnificently!

DULAN'S WIFE Couldn't you think of some other work for them than sitting and mourning alongside cheap whores!

DULAN Hold your tongue. A job's a job. You two come along, I'll take you there. The better the mourners, the more the malik's prestige increases.

SANICHARI What will people say, Dulan?

BIKHNI   Are people going to come and feed us, support us? [*To DULAN*] Come, Dulan, I'm ready to go.

SANICHARI   But... Bikhni...

BIKHNI   Shush. Go on, old man, tell us when you'll take us along.

DULAN   I'll come to fetch you in the afternoon. Be sure to wear black. And listen, Sanichari – I want my share of your earnings from any job I arrange for you.

SANICHARI   You so-and-so, you want a cut, do you!

DULAN   So what's wrong with that? Everyone from the Prime Minister down to the lowest untouchable takes cuts.

BIKHNI   A hundred bastards must have died to give birth to a rascal like you...

[*Lights off*]

Atomic Jaya

by Huzir Sulaiman

Cast

(in order of appearance)

    Dr. Mary Yuen

    Dr. Ramachandran

    Dr. Saiful

    General Zulkifli

    A BBC Newsreader

    Madeleine Albright, US Secretary of State

    A Cabinet Minister

    A RTM reporter

8 Speaking parts. All parts may be doubled.

The Setting

The scenes which occur in this play extract take place in Malaysia in the late 1990's. Act One Scenes 9, 10 and 11, take place in a variety of settings including: the home of Chinese physicist, Dr. Mary Yuen, the secret military-run laboratory at the Atomic Jaya Facility where Mary works, an office in the Atomic Jaya Facility, a BBC, (British Broadcasting Corporation) television studio, Madeleine Albright's office, and the office of a Cabinet Minister of the Malaysian parliament.

The Extract

In this satirical play, Dr. Mary Yeun documents her involvement in the development of a nuclear bomb for the Malaysian government. When the scene begins her work on the project with fellow Indian physicist, Dr. Ramachandran, and Malay physicist, Dr. Saiful is at a delicate stage.

Scene 9

[*Spotlight on YUEN. She speaks to audience.*]

YUEN   I was beginning to think I was the only one on the planet who had moral doubts about the project. But it seemed that I had company.

[*Lights. The laboratory. A delicate experiment is underway.*]

YUEN   Dr. Ramachandran?

RAMACHANDRAN   [*Absently*] Mm.

YUEN   Be careful with that canister, please.

RAMACHANDRAN   Mm. Sorry. What is it, Dr. Yuen? Anything?

YUEN   Are you all right, Dr. Ramachandran? Now is not the time for your mind to be elsewhere.

RAMACHANDRAN   Dr. Yuen, I must relate to you the story of the incident last night.

YUEN   Perhaps you could complete the transfer first? It's not a good idea to be waving... look, please be careful.

RAMACHANDRAN   It's my wife. Perhaps you will understand because you yourself are once, twice, three times a lady. Usha and I – Dr. Usha Nair, she's a medical doctor – we had a bit of an altercation. She's a very lively sort. Brimming with vitality and all that. It was a love match. We met at Iyengar's wedding. Our parents introduced us but essentially it was a love match. I think of marriage as a partnership between two equals. Or equivalents. She's the physician and I'm the physicist.

YUEN   Perhaps the physicist could assist his colleague by securing the material properly?

RAMACHANDRAN   Last night we were watching the news, Usha and I. Apparently there was a hullaballoo outside here, the Atomic Jaya Sendirian Etcetera, with demonstrators. They were showing footages and all that. These flers were chanting and shouting and carrying on. I thought, thank God the police were there, otherwise what an ugly situation. Stepped in to restore law and order and all. Used the air freshener, whatever. Okay. But Usha – Dr. Usha Nair, she's a medical – Usha wanted to take umbrage. I thought to myself, if you want to take umbrage, make sure this taking of umbrage is correct and proper. Umbrage cannot simply be taken at whim or whimsy. You will waste the umbrage. Making a mockery. 'Why is it you are building bombs? Can you furnish me with one good reason?' she said like that.

YUEN	What did you say?
RAMACHANDRAN	'We are building it for the good of the country,' I said.
YUEN	It would do the country more good if you didn't wave...
RAMACHANDRAN	At that particular point she developed a strangeness. I couldn't understand the thread of her logic. The fairer sex is completely. 'What is it for, this building bombs business? If it is potency symbol that you desire, go and build a stone lingam in the garden, I won't stop you.'
YUEN	Dr. Ramachandran. Put the materials down.
RAMACHANDRAN	I wanted to reason with her but she was oblivious. Completely oblivious.
YUEN	DR. RAMACHANDRAN! SECURE THE MATERIAL RIGHT NOW!
RAMACHANDRAN	[*Pause*] Just because you are graduate of American university is not a reason for this high-and-mighty.
YUEN	Dr. Ramachandran, we're talking basic safety here. It's not enough to wear the suits. Remember what happened to Dr. Saiful?
RAMACHANDRAN	You are suggesting I don't know what I am doing?
YUEN	No, Dr. Ramachandran. I'm doing nothing of the kind.
RAMACHANDRAN	And the next minute what is it you'll be insulting? My qualifications? PhD, madam! Honestly earned, I tell you, unlike that MIC fler, all paid for from the catalogue. How many years of struggle, I tell you. And my wife. And Usha. Medical doctor qualifications are not two a penny whatever.
YUEN	Please, Dr. Ramachandran, calm down.

RAMACHANDRAN	'Build a stone lingam in the garden.' That is what she said. She kept asking, 'Why is it we are doing this? What is the point?' Dr. Mary... I also don't know.

[*SAIFUL enters.*]

YUEN	Ah, Dr. Saiful, come in. Could you secure the material that Dr. Ramachandran is waving around?
SAIFUL	Dr. Ramachandran, you can hand me the thing.
RAMACHANDRAN	'What is the point? What is the meaning? Why are you doing this?'
SAIFUL	Oh, you are discussing philosophy. Philosophy is different. Very interesting. For example, *Men are from Besut, Women are from Dungun.* I also like philosophy.

[*Spotlight on YUEN. She speaks to audience.*]

YUEN	Ethics and recriminations and moral dilemmas. I'm a good Malaysian, I used to think; I shouldn't dwell on all the murk of our souls. Don't dig too deep. But Dr. Ramachandran was right to ask: why?
	The American physicist J. Robert Oppenheimer, who was in charge of the Manhattan Project at Los Alamos during World War 2, the American effort to build the bomb – when he saw the fireball and the mushroom cloud from the first test rising above the New Mexico desert, he was reminded of a line from the Bhagavad-Gita: 'I am become death, the eater of worlds.'
	A world is a big thing to eat. I decided to stick with being Mary Yuen, the eater of *popiah*.

Scene 10

[*The Atomic Jaya facility*]

SAIFUL	General, you have called us for a meeting, is it?
GENERAL	I am not very satisfied with the progress. I think the time has come for us to test the device.
SAIFUL	Oh, test the device? Oh. You want to test?

RAMACHANDRAN	I am afraid that if we are having Test matches now we will all be bowled out for duck. You will put us into a very sticky wicket situation.
GENERAL	India and Pakistan can do it.
RAMACHANDRAN	But General, how long has been their innings! And furthermore the pitch is very large!
GENERAL	Dr. Ramachandran, I don't understand you sometimes. Dr. Mary Yuen? I trust your opinion. You are my Marshal Murat. The only one who used tu and not vous with the Emperor of the French.
YUEN	Well, I'd like to draw your imperial majesty's attention to, one, the fact there appears to be little pressing reason to test the device at all, and two, the fact that there is nowhere in Malaysia to test a weapon this destructive.
GENERAL	I will answer point by point. One, the pressing reason is that we wish to host the Olympic Games.
YUEN	What, and nuclear warfare is now a medal event? Or is it just an exhibition sport?
SAIFUL	Taekwondo is an exhibition event. Last time. But now medal. I think so yes. So same, lah.
GENERAL	Dr. Mary Yuen, the pressing reason is because I say so. Two, we can test. We find a *padang*.
RAMACHANDRAN	No, all the calculations have been done. It is quite powerful. About 10,000 tons of TNT equivalent. The Hiroshima bomb was about 12,000 tons.
SAIFUL	It's the same. Ten, twelve. Eleven, lah, eleven. Consensus.
GENERAL	Twelve thousand tons means what?
YUEN	The damage would be enormous. The atomic bomb is lethal for three reasons: heat, blast, and radiation. There's an enormous flash of searing heat, then a pulverising shockwave, then deadly poisoning radioactivity. Let's put it this way. If you detonated the device on the Selangor Club Padang, you would have total devastation in a circle with a 2 km radius. To the East, until Lot 10. To the North, until the UMNO Building. To the West, past Parliament. And to the South, to the Brickfields YMCA.

RAMACHANDRAN	YMCA! I used to use the tennis courts there. There is a very good ikan bakar shop nearby.
SAIFUL	Not just the ikan become bakar. The whole shophouse.
YUEN	KL would be on fire. Depending on the winds and the weather, people until Damansara Heights would later die of radiation poisoning. And this is a primitive device, General. American nuclear artillery shells now carry the same payload. Their missiles are 80 times as powerful. We're talking apocalypse, General.
GENERAL	I see. That is quite serious.
YUEN	Okay. Or let's detonate our little gadget in the suburbs. In PJ, let's say, at the Cold Storage in Section 14. You would kill every single person in Sections 7, 8, 10, 11, 12, 13, 14, 16, 17, 17A, 19, 51, 51 A, 52, SSI, and SS2, and a great number in the rest of PJ.
SAIFUL	Why PJ the number so funny? I never understand.
RAMACHANDRAN	Because they don't want you to go there. PJ very closed. No foreigners.
GENERAL	That is very powerful.
YUEN	We're not like other countries. We don't have uninhabited deserts or remote atolls where we can blow up things unimpeded.
GENERAL	Borneo? There is Borneo. Sabah-Sarawak.
RAMACHANDRAN	They don't even consider themselves Malaysian. They should get a stiff reminder.
SAIFUL	They are in a different time zone. Out of step.
GENERAL	Furthermore we have the Bakun area. Seventy thousand hectares, the size of Singapore. They were going to flood it anyway. Flood, burn, it's the same. The area has been earmarked for eradication, we can eradicate. Just because the government got no money doesn't mean we want to shake legs only.
RAMACHANDRAN	If you shake your legs, the ball will strike the wicket.
YUEN	And you'll be out. You'll be bloody well knocked far the fuck out.

Scene 11

[*Spotlight on YUEN. She speaks to audience.*]

YUEN   Heisenberg's Uncertainty Principle. If you want to determine the position AND the momentum of an electron, you have a problem. You can't. Get a reading on the position, and the momentum changes. Get a reading on the momentum, and you can't fix the position. The act of observation changes that which is being observed, said Heisenberg. A good thing to remember. Something happened, but the fact that I noticed those things happening means something else happened instead. Keep that in mind. This is the point in the narrative where my point of view starts getting questionable. I'll give you a hint. Second rule of storytelling (I just remembered it): you can never be too obvious. So here goes. I did it. I sabotaged the device.

'What? What?'

One more time: I made sure it wouldn't work. Later, if I can calm down a little, and have a cup of coffee, I'll tell you how. And why. But first things first. The Americans were getting upset.

[*Blackout.*]

BBC (VO)   The United States today repeated its warning to the Malaysian government to immediately cease plans to test the low-yield atomic weapons that it is developing. Speaking at a press conference in Washington following a meeting with the Malaysian Ambassador described as 'tense and unproductive,' US Secretary of State Madeleine Albright reiterated the United States policy of zero tolerance for the continued proliferation of weapons of mass destruction.

[*Lights up on ALBRIGHT*]

ALBRIGHT   There will be serious consequences if Malaysia detonates an atomic device. The United States stands by its policy to punish those nations who arbitrarily assume nuclear powers, who contribute to the growing global nuclear arms menace. We have the might, and we have the right, and we will not hesitate to fight for the right to our might, and our might alone. We want to remind the people of Malaysia of the words of a great American president, who said, 'Ask not what your country can do for you; rather ask what our country can do to your country.'

[*Lights up on the Minister.*]

MINISTER   The United States should not meddle in the internal affairs of our country. First they want to attack our currency, make us poor. Now they want to tell us what to do. They think they can tell the Malaysian don't have the bomb. They think they can tell the Pakistan don't have the bomb. Why don't they listen when we tell them don't have the bomb? The Malaysian people are loyal. They are patriotic. When we play the national anthem they stand up. They will listen to the wisdom of their leaders and not these foreign meddlers.

[*Blackout*]

RTM (VO)   He was speaking to reporters after speaking to other reporters.

[*Spotlight on Yuen. She speaks to audience.*]

YUEN   I'm not very trustworthy you know. I make no guarantees of... I'm a little mixed up. Nonetheless.

How to sabotage an atomic bomb when you are the only person who really knows what they are doing. Step 1: Make sure the explosive charge that is supposed to drive the uranium bullet into the uranium block is not sufficient to drive the uranium bullet into the uranium block. Step 2: Make sure that the explosive charge instead fractures the tube so that the two blocks of uranium fall away separately and are lost. Step 3: Falsify the test results like there's no tomorrow. Step 4: Hope you don't get caught.

The Pohutukawa Tree

by Bruce Mason

CAST

(in order of appearance)

    Johnny Mataira

    Aroha Mataira

    Queenie Mataira

    Rev. Athol Sedgwick

    Roy McDowell

5 Speaking parts. No doubling.

The Setting

The scene, which occurs during Act Two, Scene One, takes place in the modest living room of the Mataira house situated in a New Zealand farming district called Te Parenga during the Autumn of 1947. The living room belongs to Mrs Aroha Mataira, a widow in her sixties and proud Maori chieftaness. The Pohutukawa tree hangs low over the doorway to the porch. There is a fireplace, a battered sofa, a table and two chairs in the room as well as two portraits; Holman Hunt's 'The Light of the World' and a photograph of the tattooed Maori chief, and Mataira ancestor, Whetumarama. A fruit bowl with grapefruit in it together with a copy of the family Bible sits on the table.

The Extract

Queenie's older brother, Johnny, is dressed in his orchard working clothes. At the start of the scene he searches the fruit bowl for the best grapefruit to give to his mother. Queenie, aged seventeen, sits on a chair looking wild and distracted.

JOHNNY	Hi, Queenie. You all right? Ma! Queenie's back!
	[*He searches among the grapefruit. AROHA appears at the door.*]
AROHA	You were a long time, Queenie… What's the matter?
	[*QUEENIE puts her head in her hands.*]
AROHA	[*Going to her*] Queenie! Queenie, girl. Something's happened.
QUEENIE	[*Piteously*] Ma!
AROHA	[*Agitated*] Something happened with Dr Lomas. Yes?
	[*QUEENIE nods.*]
	Are you ill?
	[*QUEENIE shakes her head, stops, nods.*]
	What do you mean? Tell me, Queenie!
	[*QUEENIE is still silent. AROHA pulls her to her feet.*]
QUEENIE	Tell me!
	[*QUEENIE cannot say the words; tries but cannot. AROHA comprehends.*]
	[*A long pause. AROHA and JOHNNY stand rigid. QUEENIE slowly sits.*]
AROHA	Whose. Whose!
QUEENIE	Roy McDowell's.
AROHA	Who is he? Johnny: do you know him?
JOHNNY	Chap at the pub.
AROHA	Pakeha?
	[*JOHNNY nods.*]
AROHA	Go and get him. At once. And bring Mr Sedgwick, too. Straight away, now!
	[*JOHNNY dives out.*]
AROHA	When did this happen?
QUEENIE	Three months ago.
AROHA	Often?
QUEENIE	Yes.
AROHA	Where?

QUEENIE	Up there. In the bush.
AROHA	When?
QUEENIE	After you had gone to bed.
AROHA	Slut. Slut!
QUEENIE	[*Angry*] Don't say things like that, Ma!
AROHA	My daughter. The great granddaughter of Whetu-marama. Reared in Christ. Taught to respect her past and her race and the sacred ground of Ngati-Raukura.

And she uses it for that!... That!

QUEENIE	Yes, for that! For love!
AROHA	Love. Love!
QUEENIE	[*Passionately*] You don't know what love is. All wrapped up in Whetumarama and Him up there. I'm sick of it, sick of it. Rammed down my throat every day. It doesn't mean a thing! And I'll do it again, Ma. I will, I will, I will!

[*AROHA slaps her savagely across the mouth. QUEENIE cries out.*]

QUEENIE	[*Slowly*] Don't you hit me, Ma. I'm having a baby.

[*AROHA stares at her.*]

AROHA	How old is he?
QUEENIE	Twenty-one.
AROHA	A baby, just a baby. And do you like him, this baby of yours?
QUEENIE	[*Hurt*] I like him okay.
AROHA	'I like him okay.' A love speech, eh Queenie? Yes, yes. You know what love is.
QUEENIE	I don't care what you think. It's my life.
AROHA	Not till you're twenty-one, my girl. You want to marry this boy?
QUEENIE	Course I do.
AROHA	I can stop you, Queenie.
QUEENIE	[*Shrewdly*] You won't do that.
AROHA	Why won't I?
QUEENIE	What about the Atkinsons?
AROHA	Don't mention their name! You've brought shame on me and shame on them, who've been so good to you.

QUEENIE   Then I'd better get married; quick too, eh Ma?

AROHA   [*Heavily*] Yes. Yes. Yes, you'll get married. Yes, you'll go away with him somewhere, far away from here. Forget everything I've taught you. And when your child's born, there'll be another and another and another. A dozen of them, all crying for food – and if your man goes on the way he's started with you, there'll be other women to take your place when you're fat and ugly. All your life, I've tried to bring you up straight and clean. Teach you honour, respect, pride. You're pretty: you could have had a fine husband when you moved out into the world. But you go and fall for the first no-good pakeha that comes along. Weak. Weak. After all my teaching. All right: that's your life. Now go and enjoy it.

QUEENIE   [*With dignity*] Perhaps I will, Ma. Perhaps I won't worry all the time what the pakeha thinks of me. Perhaps I won't look ahead all the time, like you do. And perhaps, if I'm happy today, I won't be thinking about what tomorrow will bring. And then perhaps, tomorrow won't be so bad.

   [*A pause*]

AROHA   Queenie, Queenie! Why did you do it?

QUEENIE   Because I wanted to. That's why.

AROHA   Couldn't you have come to me?

QUEENIE   [*Scornful, yet pitying*] Ma. Oh, Ma! ... When will I get married?

AROHA   [*Grimly*] Tomorrow, my girl. Tomorrow.

QUEENIE   But what about my dress?

AROHA   What dress?

QUEENIE   My wedding dress, Ma!

AROHA   What!

QUEENIE   I want to be all in white, a crown on my head.

AROHA   Queenie girl: have you gone out of your senses? Mr Sedgwick can't marry you in white.

QUEENIE   But why?

AROHA   A bride is untouched. You are not.

QUEENIE   I'll ask Mr Sedgwick.

AROHA   He'll say no.

QUEENIE   I'll ask him.

AROHA	[*Shouting*] Ask then! But I know his answer.
	[*She looks at QUEENIE and her face twitches. She turns away to hide a smile, sits down on the sofa, suddenly quite calm.*]
QUEENIE	[*Coming up to her*] Can't I have just a little orange blossom in my hair? Make me smell nice?
	[*AROHA laughs suddenly.*]
AROHA	Vanity, vanity, all is vanity. All right. Ask the Minister. See what he says.
	[*QUEENIE sits on the floor beside AROHA.*]
QUEENIE	I think you'll like Roy, Ma.
AROHA	He'd better be nice.
QUEENIE	He loves me a lot. Said so, dozens of times.
AROHA	That's something, then.
QUEENIE	You've seen him, Ma. At the wedding.
AROHA	[*Unfavourably impressed*] That boy!
QUEENIE	Oh, I know he looks a bit tough. But he's not like that really. I know, you see.
AROHA	[*Turning to look at her*] You wicked girl.
QUEENIE	Yes, I am. I'm wicked. But I like it, Ma.
AROHA	[*Gently*] Hold your tongue.
	[*The sound of the men approaching. JOHNNY arrives with SEDGWICK and ROY. JOHNNY stands aside for SEDGWICK to enter. ROY stands outside in an extremity of embarrassment.*]
SEDGWICK	[*Beckoning him in*] This is Roy McDowell, Mrs Mataira.
	[*AROHA looks at him carefully.*]
SEDGWICK	Well, it looks as if I have the floor. Queenie is expecting a child and Roy admits to being the father. Right?
ROY	Yeh. So far.
SEDGWICK	Well, these things have happened before and no doubt they'll happen again. With a little understanding we can sort it all out. Now: answer me honestly. Has this sort of thing happened to you before?
ROY	Not this way, it hasn't.

SEDGWICK	All right, then. Well, obviously the first thing for you to do is get married as soon as possible. I can get a special licence and marry you the day after tomorrow. How's that?
QUEENIE	Mr Sedgwick?
SEDGWICK	Yes. Queenie?
QUEENIE	Can I wear a white dress? With a veil and a crown?
SEDGWICK	You mean: dress as a bride?
QUEENIE	Yes. With orange blossom.
SEDGWICK	No, Queenie. I'm afraid you can't. Not in my Church. A rule's a rule, and I'm going to stick to it.
QUEENIE	Oh, don't give me that. It's only a show, the Church stuff. If I'm going to be married, I want my show too. I want lots of people and everybody looking at me, saying, see that girl up there: that's Queenie Mataira, isn't she lovely. You'll hear 'Here comes the Bride', and I'll be on Mr Atkinson's arm; he always said he'd give me away…
SEDGWICK	I'm afraid Mr Atkinson might feel a little differently…
AROHA	None of this must even get to Mr Atkinson! He won't give you away: how could he?
QUEENIE	What's it to him? I'm getting married, aren't I? I'm still me, aren't I? What's changed about that?
AROHA	[*Fiercely*] There will be no guests, understand? No guests, no music, no Atkinsons, no party. And you will go away as soon as it is over.
QUEENIE	Where to?
AROHA	That's for your husband to say.
	[*All look at ROY.*]
ROY	There's just one thing you're all forgetting. Me.
SEDGWICK	What do you mean?
ROY	[*Acting tough*] It's pretty clear what I mean, isn't it?
QUEENIE	Roy!
AROHA	You got my daughter into trouble. You marry her now and give her your name.
SEDGWICK	It's the honourable thing to do.
ROY	Yeh? Well, maybe I'm not so honourable… You've all taken it for granted. Well, I'd just like to let you know that it's not

cut and dried, that's all. I don't have to marry Queenie. There's no law says I have to.

QUEENIE   [*Appealingly*] But you will, Roy, won't you? You will, won't you?

ROY   [*Gently*] I can't, Queenie.

QUEENIE   Roy!

AROHA   Why?

ROY   I just can't, that's all.

SEDGWICK   You'll have to make some explanation, young man. You can't just leave it at that.

ROY   You can't force me to marry and you can't force me to talk about it.

QUEENIE   Don't you love me, Roy? That what it is?

ROY   [*Troubled*] You know I'm fond of you, Queenie. More than any...You know that.

QUEENIE   Then what is it? Roy: tell me.

ROY   [*Lamely*] You're too young. You're only seventeen.

AROHA   She has my consent. I don't want to give it, but I give it.

[*Silence*]

SEDGWICK   Look, young man. I know you don't go to Church or abide by its commandments. I know what you think of parsons. Killjoys, aren't we? Always stopping people having fun. Well, you've got to pay for fun. And that's where we Bible-banging drearies come in. To show you where fun ends and responsibility begins. And it's my job to show you where your duty lies –

ROY   Aw, don't give me that –

SEDGWICK   Don't interrupt me, please! It's quite clear what you must do. This girl will bear your child and you must acknowledge it by marriage. That's all there is to it.

ROY   [*Slowly*] That's all there is to it. All right you've asked for it. Queenie's a Maori, don't you understand?

SEDGWICK   I know she's a Maori. Well?

ROY   How can I take her home with me? What will my folks say?

SEDGWICK   You should have thought of that before.

ROY   It'd be a mixed marriage. Brown kids! I couldn't have brown kids!

SEDGWICK   You'll be the father of one. And anyway, I'm told this
           country's full of mixed marriages. Good ones, too.

ROY   [*Urgently*] Aw, but you don't know my folks. My Dad'd have
           a fit! And Mum: you don't know Mum. I just don't know
           what she'd say: she hates anything like this! She wouldn't
           have Queenie in the house.

           I know she wouldn't! Her friends'd cut her dead! And I'm
           young: I've got my life before me! You've got to think of
           that! ...I like the Maoris, always have, don't believe in colour
           bar, but... well, marriage is different, that's all... It
           shouldn't have happened! It shouldn't have happened!

SEDGWICK   No, you're quite right: it shouldn't. But it's too late now.

ROY   I can't, I can't, I can't! It wouldn't be fair on Queenie!

           [*AROHA rises with majestic calm.*]

AROHA   What are your parents?

ROY   My Dad's a grocer.

AROHA   A grocer. Is that so high and mighty, then?

ROY   No. They're good folks. Nothing special, I suppose, but
           they're my folks.

AROHA   Do you know that Queen ie comes from a long line of chiefs?
           That she can trace her ancestors through twenty-five
           generations of Ngati-Raukura?

ROY   Yeh. She told me.

AROHA   Is that not good enough for your mother?

ROY   Aw, what does it matter to my Mum that Queenie comes
           from a long line of chiefs? She'd just be a Maori to her. Look,
           Mrs Mataira. You can't live on that stuff now. Okay before
           the white man came, but now: well, this is a white man's
           country now.

Ka Shue (Letters Home)

by Lynda Chanwai-Earle

Cast

(in order of appearance)
   Jackie
   Abbie
   Ghost
   Paw Paw
5 Speaking parts. All parts may be doubled by one actress.

Setting

The scenes, which occur in Acts One and Two, take place in a variety of settings and time frames including: Tiananmen Square, China, in 1989, Abbie's living-room in Wellington, New Zealand, in 1989, a lawyer's office in Wellington in 959, the ghost's realm in China, Paw Paw's house in Hong Kong in 1941, Nigel's student flat in Wellington in 1959, and the Leung family kitchen in Wellington in 1959.

The Extract

During the 1989 Chinese democracy riots, Jackie sits in her hotel in Tiananmen Square reading a letter from her mother, Abbie, about her grandmother, Paw Paw's, outrageous behaviour in the past at a family dinner. She pieces together the intergenerational stories of her Chinese / New Zealand family that have brought her to this place.

Act Two

Scene 8

[*Tiananmen, June 3, 1989, 10 pm. The hotel room. JACKIE paces, looking out the window. She speaks directly to the audience.*]

JACKIE   [*Anxiously*] They've come from all directions, since 6 o'clock tonight. They don't look friendly. They've got assault rifles. Convoys. That's what Paul said – military convoys. [*Pause*] God, where is he? [*Re-assuring*] I'm sure he'll be alright. Never gone out with a boy like him. A real sweetie though. [*Laughs*]

My mother can't stand Chinese men, and she's Chinese!

[*She reads out the letter, imitating ABBIE.*]

'Your father wants to know how many letters you've sent me. I think you'd better write him more. He's worried about you, Jackie and I really don't know about you and this Paul. You know, Chinese men, they don't make good lovers, they only care about money and their bodies... they're like little girls! [*Incredulous*] Chinese men don't make good lovers? What about Pakeha ones? 'Not trust guilo as far as throw him,' says Paw paw. And what does my mother do? She married one. And what'd he do? He left her. [*Recalls*] They all turned up for my farewell dinner... God what a night! It started off okay – except for Paw paw hissing in my ear 'Guilo bring guipo!' We're in this restaurant. All dressed up. Sitting in a big circle. Very polite. Mum on one side. Paw paw on the other. Across the table Janet and Dad. Janet – she's not much older than me. So there we are, sitting round smiling... bit like chimpanzees. They grimace when they're frightened. 'The little girl's grown up. Time for the big O.E.' . Dad's got his home video, sticking the camera in my face! Then he shoves it right onto Paw paw: 'Smile to the camera Mamee', first she hisses at him. 'Not call me Mamee', but its like he's got a death wish or something. 'Go on Mamee, talk to the little birdie. Tell us what you think about Jackie going away... Janet wants to know too, don't you Janet?' That was it!

[*JACKIE picks up the knife from the floor.*]

Paw paw starts waving this knife around. 'You bring shame to Abbie! I kill you, I kill you!' Next thing there's plates and glasses flying everywhere, and I'm holding onto her trying to get the knife! I tell you for a sixty-eight-year-old she's got a hell of a grip! And there's Janet. White as a ghost. Mumbles some excuse and scarpers. Flees the scene.

[*JACKIE laughs, picking up the knife and placing it on the chest.*]

Poor Dad! Some farewell... Even offered to foot the bill for the breakages.

[*Lights and music change, scene shifts to:*]

Scene 9

[*Wellington, June 1989. ABBIE's sitting room, the moment following the end of her last scene. ABBIE continues speaking into her dictaphone to JACKIE who is in China.*]

ABBIE   [*Laughs*] The trouble with us Chinese is that we're supposed to be inscrutable – you never know what we're thinking, what we're going to do next. When I was sixteen I ran away from home. And your grandfather tracked me down. I was staying with my pakeha girlfriend, Charlene. Babaa had this man with him, a market gardener. He knew I hated him. He was like a peasant. The kind that blew his [*Disgust*] snot onto his shirt sleeve! Brought him anyway. Like back-up. Poor Charlene. She opened the door and Babaa just stormed in. [*Incredulous*] Spat in my face! Then he hugged me. The first time he'd touched me since I was little. [*Pause, then with difficulty*] He started to cry. Actually crying... He was going on about how I was a .. his little baby girl, his piano baby. I had to stand there letting him hold me, while this stupid man, this stupid peasant said things to me. Hissed at me. How... how ungrateful! You bring shame! ... recriminations... things.

[*ABBIE recovers herself, laughing, embarrassed.*]

Don't know why I'm telling you this... I – Damn!

[*ABBIE turns off the dictaphone, disconcerted.*]

Lawyer's office ... Wellington, 1959 ... I was so young.

[*Lights and music change, scene shifts to:*]

Scene 10

[*Wellington 1959. ABBIE is speaking to her lawyer. (She directs her speech out to the audience.)*]

ABBIE   My mother calls me a slut. You don't believe me do you? Yes, my own mother! [*Pause*] Yes my parents are respectable, law abiding citizens but... I came to you Mr Wrightson because you're Charlene's father.

She said you could help, everyone says you're a great lawyer... I'm aware that this doesn't look good for the community but I need protection... Yes, I'm 21 now... No, my father doesn't hit me frequently. Bruises? No... It's not quite like that... it's more subtle... He threatens me. He wants to know everything. Who I see, what I do... I don't want to stir up trouble, [*Frustrated*] No I can't talk to anyone else. It's a small community. They all think my parents are – honourable... It'll bring shame to... I want to leave. Please can you speak to them? I'm old enough to live my own life ... I want to marry Nigel. I don't care that he's white. [*Pause*] Sorry... but if my father finds out I'm telling you this... I just want to be free!

[*ABBIE suddenly looks to the side shocked.*]

Babaa? – What are you doing here? No... no!

[*She falls back as if struck. Lights and music change, scene shifts to:*]

Scene 11

[*The silhouette of the Ghost appears, back-lit in a shimmering pool of light. She continues the legend. Peking opera sounds swell around her.*]

GHOST
Poverty is the greatest violence, The Chinese character for money is compose of three symbol. One is gold. The other two represent spear. The character for poverty is also compose of three symbol. The symbol depict a man standing at the bottom of pit, bent as if under great burden.

[*The GHOST becomes CHONG ER, her hands are outstretched as before, she devours the soup.*]

Chong Er devoured his soup ravenously. Recovering his strength [*Holds hand out*]... he ask his men, 'Where did meat come from?' The men looked at Jie Zitui: his gown is stain with blood. Chong Er so happy he embrace Jie Zitui... 'What shall I do to repay you?' Jie Zitui reply, 'You have taste the full bitterness of the people through this exile. I wish you only be King clear and bright in future.'

[*Lights and music change, scene shifts to:*]

Scene 12

[*Hong Kong 1941. Sudden dramatic darkness and exploding sounds, a scream. Sounds of the approaching Japanese invasion without. As the lights come up PAW PAW is clutching ABBIE (the mock-up baby in swaddling) who is only a few months old. She is panicking, trying to stop ABBIE's crying while making the motions of packing, using the long red cloths as if one were a sack and the others mere items of clothing. She has misplaced her precious family heirloom, the gold chain and locket. PAW PAW searches desperately while directing her speech to the baby. At the end of the scene we find the heirloom is in her pocket all along.*]

PAW PAW   Good luck, is what you need. A lot of it. How I suppose to get you out? Not even Kuomintang save us now.

[*She stops packing to search for the gold.*]

It all because of you! My husband say I not go to New Zealand unless I bring you. Here we are, stuck in Hong Kong and Japanese invasion! All because of you! Abbie, Abbie - what stupid name for baby! [*To herself*] Was not safe before. So hide it again. I put in here I know. 1941 – not good year. Year of Snake. No wonder there so much trouble. War everywhere. I put it – where? Where? [*Screams*] Shut up! You lucky you bless with me. [*Pause*] He always have soft spot for your mother, Lady Li. She was nothing, nothing but concubine! I am First wife, me!

[*She now directs her venom at baby ABBIE.*]

Wishee you die with her, wishee she jump down well with you inside her stomach! Till na ma!

[*She lunges for the baby's throat but stops short, breathing heavily.*]

Never mind. You help me work in fruit shop.

[*She begins her search for the locket again.*]

Lucky you bless with me. If leave you here, maybe Japanese man eat you. That what Ma say. Japanese men like eat baby. You lucky I take you. Yes.

[*The sound of approaching gun fire gets louder as do ABBIE's cries. Paw paw is distracted as she hurries through belongings, tossing things everywhere, looking for her gold locket.*]

Maybe I send you for school, maybe. Take my son Cyril. And you. [*Angry*] Cyril cry for his father. He good boy. He only little. My husband not need hit him so hard. I give him son but he like you more because you hers. Shut up! ... Can't find it! You repay me. Look after me and Babaa. Repay debt. Be good daughter. Least I can walk. Not like some women. With golden lily feet. Japanese probably rape them. Me! I can run!

[*She finds her gold, hugely relieved.*]

Oh! Yes ... Daw geh! Daw geh! Now we go...

[*She searches for a new place to hide the gold.*]

Where they not find?

[*She places the gold into the baby's napkin.*]

Maybe they not look for it in here. Mix blessing. Story of my life. Mix blessing.

[*She suddenly remembers Cyril, her son, and the Amah, and calls out to them, off-stage.*]

Cyril? Cyril! Amah! Come. Quick!

[*Lights and music change, end act one.*]

ACT TWO

Scene 1

[*Wellington 1959, Nigel's student flat. ABBIE is arguing with PAW PAW over the telephone.*]

ABBIE   I'm not coming home ...

I'm not coming home. I'm going to live... [*Suspicious*] Yes, I am at Nigel's flat... I'm not coming... Listen Mamee

He's not a Communist for god's sake, he's a student! It's 1959 Mamee, things are different... It's not like that ... Nigel's not that sort of person! Mamee... Ma ... listen to ... Mamee listen to me, we're getting ... We're getting married!... Mamee [*Mutters*] I couldn't feel more lucid actually... No... lucid's not a drug – oh never mind. Aunty Ying came around... Aunty Ying! She was being insufferable... No I'm not swearing... Nigel says the Chinese community are frightened... from years of [*Trails off*] oppression... what? [*Shocked silence*] No!... No!!

[*PAW PAW hangs up on the other end. ABBIE places the receiver down, fuming.*]

Okay – Fine!

[*Lights and mime change, scene shifts to:*]

Scene 2

[*The GHOST is centre up-stage, under the headpiece.*]

GHOST   Nineteen years after his exile Chong Er become Emperor of China. After ascend throne, he confer title and award to meritorious official who follow him in exile, only to forget Jie Zitui ... Many people angry at injustice done to Jie, advise him to see Chong Er, ask for reward. Jie Zitui however refuse contend for merit. Instead, he quietly got things ready, went to Mianshang Mountain to live in seclusion, carrying his old mother upon his back.

[*Lights and music change, scene shifts to*:]

Scene 3

[*Wellington, 1959, the Leung family kitchen. PAW PAW is arguing with young ABBIE over the telephone. She breaks in and out of English and Cantonese. On the chest is the rice bowl with chopsticks.*]

PAW PAW   [*Polite*] Abbie?... Ah. You think so? You think maybe you stay with him? [*Pause*] You run away now?... Ah, but you at his place?... Oh do not bother on behalf of us. We just silly old Chinese people, [*Cold*] Just wait till Babaa find out! You stupid girl. Abbie – a guilo! [*Laughs*] With no money. Aiyee! A Communist too, eh? Probably he is! You give us bad name. Not care about family?... Selfish child. We send you to good school. What you do for us, eh? You thanking us by sleeping with guilo! You so stupid. He leave you. I know. He leave you for other white girl, [*Shocked pause*] You mahlee... You mahlee?... You want I die? You must be outa your mind!... Lucid? Now you tell me you on drug too? I curse you ... What you say? Who?... Why you swearing about at Aunty Ying?... Is rubbish!... See! Communist!... All guilo want is... is... to make fuck with you. You think he wanna mahlee you? You got be choking! He mahlee you for our money that all! Don't think you can put your face round here! You not come home – no, no! Never come home now! You are... are... slut! [*Spits*] See Mung Nui! [*Tries to compose herself*] Abbie you come back or I tell Babaa. He cut you allowance! You leave – got no money – you die, starve to death! [*Tearful*] All my children so selfish. Not care how hard they make my life! [*Suddenly cold*] I tell Babaa! He get you, give you proper beating! [*Venomous*] Proper beating!

[*PAW PAW hangs up on ABBIE, fumes for a moment then picks up her bowl of rice and begins to eat, calming herself.*]

It dark when I wake. Put on woollen singlet. Corset. Thick
stocking. Keep leg warm. Bloomer. Old cheongsam. Put on
my sock. Three pair these day. Black glove, no finger. Better
for pick up fruit. Go downstair and open shop. First
customer Mr Jone. He always come too early – complain
service slow. I tell him. Mr Jone 7 o'clock we open shop.
Then Mr Jone you buy banana for breakfast. I even offer
deliver. But he bit crazy. Anyway he say to me 'Have nice
day' and I give him banana. [*Pause*] When children little,
next door Parker kid rude to Cyril. Cyril just little boy then.
He good boy. This Parker kid little shit. He say to Cyril,
'Ching chong China man, eatee doggie in fry pan!' Punch
Cyril! It very hard for Cyril. He not allow fight back. Give us
bad name. [*Pause*] Guilo call us 'alien'. Say we pay one
hundred pound or not come. It take long time save, I sell
family gold, just to come! Leave Amah behind. Cyril cry for
Amah when we get on big boat. He want her come too.
Everything different here. No Amah look after children...
[*Pause*] New Zealand government not charge anyone else fee
but Chinese. They let us in New Zealand, say we be good
and only stay two year. Until war over. Then we all go
home. Back to China ... [*Angry*] Why we go back when
Japanese everywhere?

[*She pauses to eat some rice.*]

We ate pigeon from park one day. Why not? Maybe I
shoulda kill next-door Parker dog. One day stupid mutt got
one of my chicken. Mr Parker not even say sorry. [*Pause*]

Better I not. Make government unhappy – if I eat neighbour
dog. Guilos! So stupid! We only people with sense. If you
hungry just whistle and it come. No need hunt or hiss!
[*Pause*] And him. Mr Parker. He no better than a dog far as
I can see. Like my husband. Stupid man. Always drinking
and screaming at wife. My husband spend too long with
guilo. Gone to his head. My husband say, 'come over, come
over' writing letter. I in Hong Kong with Japanese Invasion,
he say, 'Come over, plenty of money here for family.
Business good.' What business? Stupid shit! No money
because he spend it all on himself at stupid hotel on stupid
mah-jong, and the woman, [*Warily*] I know he has her. This
not home. Not China. He think he can be married more than
one wife. They arrest him. If he try marry another I leave
him. He think I not know but I do. I seen him. Think I not
know. I just say nothing, [*Frustrated*] One day he want I
give school money. No way! Our children gotta go. I want
Cyril be doctor, one day. Abbie play piano. Good husband

want her if she go good school. It gotta be that way. I tell him. He say no. Kid work for business first. He start yelling. He want money bad. For debt, [*Defeated*] For long time I hold my tongue, [*Defiantly*] Then I tell him. I say No. No more for mah-jong. No more take, take, take. He say I 'bitch' or something. Say I be good to him or he go. [*With great strength*] Sure. He go. He got nothing. I work. My business.

[*PAW PAW places her bowl and chopsticks on the chest, rubbing her sore back.*]

Death and the King's Horseman

by Wole Soyinka

CAST

(in order of appearance)

    Olunde

    Jane Pilkings

    Aide-de-camp

3 Speaking parts. No doubling.

The Setting

The scene, which occurs in Scene 4 of this play, takes place in 1946 on a hot evening in a wide corridor which surrounds the great hall at the governing British Officer's Residency in Oyo, the ancient Yoruba city of Nigeria.

The Extract

A masked, costumed ball for the ex-patriotic community in honour of the visit of a British Prince takes place in the hall. Olunde, a member of the Yoruba tribal group, and eldest son of Elesin, the Horseman of the King, appears in a lounge suit in the corridor. Owing to Elesin's actions a civil emergency is underway in the city. Attending the ball is Jane Pilkings, wife of the District Officer, Simon Pilkings. Jane appears dressed for the masked ball wearing a tribal costume and a Yoruba ancestral mask. She is unaware of the effect this might have on Olunde.

OLUNDE	[*Emerging into the light*] I didn't mean to startle you madam. I am looking for the District Officer.
JANE	Wait a minute...don't I know you? Yes, you are Olunde, the young man who .. .
OLUNDE	Mrs Pilkings! How fortunate. I came here to look for your husband.
JANE	Olunde! Let's look at you. What a fine young man you've become. Grand but solemn. Good God, when did you return? Simon never said a word. But you do look well Olunde. Really!
OLUNDE	You are... well, you look quite well yourself Mrs Pilkings. From what little I can see of you.
JANE	Oh, this. It's caused quite a stir I assure you, and not all of it very pleasant. You are not shocked I hope?
OLUNDE	Why should I be? But don't you find it rather hot in there? Your skin must find it difficult to breathe.
JANE	Well, it is a little hot I must confess, but it's all in a good cause.
OLUNDE	What cause Mrs Pilkings?
JANE	All this. The ball. And His Highness being here in person and all that.
OLUNDE	[*Mildly*] And that is the good cause for which you desecrate an ancestral mask?
JANE	Oh, so you are shocked after all. How disappointing.
OLUNDE	No I am not shocked Mrs Pilkings. You forget that I have now spent four years among your people. I discovered that you have no respect for what you do not understand.
JANE	Oh. So you've returned with a chip on your shoulder. That's a pity Olunde. I am sorry.
	[*An uncomfortable silence follows.*]
	I take it then that you did not find your stay in England altogether edifying.
OLUNDE	I don't say that. I found your people quite admirable in many ways, their conduct and courage in this war for instance.
JANE	Ah yes the war. Here of course it is all rather remote. From time to time we have a blackout drill just to remind us that there is a war on. And the rare convoy passes through on its way somewhere or on manoeuvres. Mind you there is the

occasional bit of excitement like that ship that was blown up in the harbour.

OLUNDE Here? Do you mean through enemy action?

JANE Oh no, the war hasn't come that close. The captain did it himself. I don't quite understand it really. Simon tried to explain. The ship had to be blown up because it had become dangerous to the other ships, even to the city itself. Hundreds of the coastal population would have died.

OLUNDE Maybe it was loaded with ammunition and had caught fire. Or some of those lethal gases they've been experimenting on.

JANE Something like that. The captain blew himself up with it. Deliberately. Simon said someone had to remain on board to light the fuse.

OLUNDE It must have been a very short fuse.

JANE [*Shrugs*] I don't know much about it. Only that there was no other way to save lives. No time to devise anything else. The captain took the decision and carried it out.

OLUNDE Yes ... I quite believe it. I met men like that in England.

JANE Oh just look at me! Fancy welcoming you back with such morbid news. Stale too. It was at least six months ago.

OLUNDE I don't find it morbid at all. I find it rather inspiring. It is an affirmative commentary on life.

JANE What is?

OLUNDE That captain's self-sacrifice.

JANE Nonsense. Life should never be thrown deliberately away.

OLUNDE And the innocent people round the harbour?

JANE Oh, how does one know? The whole thing was probably exaggerated anyway.

OLUNDE That was a risk the captain couldn't take. But please Mrs Pilkings, do you think you could find your husband for me? I have to talk to him.

JANE Simon? Oh [*As she recollects for the first time the full significance of OLUNDE's presence*] Simon is ... there is a little problem in town. He was sent for. But... when did you arrive? Does Simon know you're here?

OLUNDE [*Suddenly earnest*] I need your help Mrs Pilkings. I've always found you somewhat more understanding than your husband. Please find him for me and when you do, you must help me talk to him.

JANE   I'm afraid I don't quite... follow you. Have you seen my
               husband already?

OLUNDE   I went to your house. Your houseboy told me you were here.
               [*He smiles.*] He even told me how I would recognize you and
               Mr Pilkings.

JANE   Then you must know what my husband is trying to do for
               you.

OLUNDE   For me?

JANE   For you. For your people. And to think he didn't even know
               you were coming back! But how do you happen to be here?
               Only this evening we were talking about you. We thought
               you were still four thousand miles away.

OLUNDE   I was sent a cable.

JANE   A cable? Who did? Simon? The business of your father didn't
               begin till tonight.

OLUNDE   A relation sent it weeks ago, and it said nothing about my
               father. All it said was, Our King is dead. But I knew I had
               to return home at once so as to bury my father. I understood
               that.

JANE   Well, thank God you don't have to go through that agony.
               Simon is going to stop it.

OLUNDE   That's why I want to see him. He's wasting his time. And
               since he has been so helpful to me I don't want him to incur
               the enmity of our people. Especially over nothing.

JANE   [*Sits down open-mouthed.*] You ... you Olunde!

OLUNDE   Mrs Pilkings, I came home to bury my father. As soon as I
               heard the news I booked my passage home. In fact we were
               fortunate. We travelled in the same convoy as your Prince,
               so we had excellent protection.

JANE   But you don"t think your father is also entitled to whatever
               protection is available to him?

OLUNDE   How can I make you understand? He has protection. No one
               can undertake what he does tonight without the deepest
               protection the mind can conceive. What can you offer him in
               place of his peace of mind, in place of the honour and
               veneration of his own people? What would you think of your
               Prince if he had refused to accept the risk of losing his life
               on this voyage? This... showing-the-flag tour of colonial
               possessions.

JANE   I see. So it isn't just medicine you studied in England.

OLUNDE   Yet another error into which your people fall. You believe that everything which appears to make sense was learnt from you.

JANE   Not so fast Olunde. You have learnt to argue, I can tell that, but I never said you made sense. However cleverly you try to put it, it is still a barbaric custom. It is even worse – it's feudal! The king dies and a chieftain must be buried with him. How feudalistic can you get!

OLUNDE   [*Waves his hand towards the background. The PRINCE is dancing past again - to a different step - and all the guests are bowing and curtseying as he passes.*] And this? Even in the midst of a devastating war, look at that. What name would you give to that?

JANE   Therapy, British style. The preservation of sanity in the midst of chaos.

OLUNDE   Others would call it decadence. However, it doesn't really interest me. You white races know how to survive; I've seen proof of that. By all logical and natural laws this war should end with all the white races wiping out one another, wiping out their so-called civilisation for all time and reverting to a state of primitivism the like of which has so far only existed in your imagination when you thought of us. I thought all that at the beginning. Then I slowly realised that your greatest art is the art of survival. But at least have the humility to let others survive in their own way.

JANE   Through ritual suicide?

OLUNDE   Is that worse than mass suicide? Mrs Pilkings, what do you call what those young men are sent to do by their generals in this war? Of course you have also mastered the art of calling things by names which don't remotely describe them.

JANE   You talk! You people with your long-winded, roundabout way of making conversation.

OLUNDE   Mrs Pilkings, whatever we do, we never suggest that a thing is the opposite of what it really is. In your newsreels I heard defeats, thorough, murderous defeats described as strategic victories. No wait, it wasn't just on your newsreels. Don't forget I was attached to hospitals all the time. Hordes of your wounded passed through those wards. I spoke to them. I spent long evenings by their bedside while they spoke terrible truths of the realities of that war. I know now how history is made.

JANE   But surely, in a war of this nature, for the morale of the nation you must expect ...

OLUNDE   That a disaster beyond human reckoning be spoken of as a triumph? No. I mean, is there no mourning in the home of the bereaved that such blasphemy is permitted?

JANE   [*After a moment's pause*] Perhaps I can understand you now. The time we picked for you was not really one for seeing us at our best.

OLUNDE   Don't think it was just the war. Before that even started I had plenty of time to study your people. I saw nothing, finally, that gave you the right to pass judgement on other peoples and their ways. Nothing at all.

JANE   [*Hesitantly*] Was it the ... colour thing? I know there is some discrimination.

OLUNDE   Don't make it so simple, Mrs Pilkings. You make it sound as if when I left, I took nothing at all with me.

JANE   Yes... and to tell the truth, only this evening, Simon and I agreed that we never really knew what you left with.

OLUNDE   Neither did I. But I found out over there. I am grateful to your country for that. And I will never give it up.

JANE   Olunde, please ... promise me something. Whatever you do, don't throw away what you have started to do. You want to be a doctor. My husband and I believe you will make an excellent one, sympathetic and competent. Don't let anything make you throw away your training.

OLUNDE   [*Genuinely surprised*] Of course not. What a strange idea. 1 intend to return and complete my training. Once the burial of my father is over.

JANE   Oh, please ...!

OLUNDE   Listen! Come outside. You can't hear anything against that music.

JANE   What is it?

OLUNDE   The drums. Can you hear the change? Listen.

            [*The drums come over, still distant but more distinct. There is a change of rhythm, it rises to a crescendo and then, suddenly, it is cut off. After a silence, a new beat begins, slow and resonant.*]

            There. It's all over.

JANE   You mean he's . . .

OLUNDE   Yes Mrs Pilkings, my father is dead. His will-power has always been enormous; I know he is dead.

JANE	[*Screams*] How can you be so callous! So unfeeling! You announce your father's own death like a surgeon looking down on some strange ... stranger's body! You're just a savage like all the rest.
AIDE-DE-CAMP	[*Rushing out*] Mrs Pilkings. Mrs Pilkings. [*She breaks down, sobbing.*] Are you alright, Mrs Pilkings?
OLUNDE	She'll be alright. [*Turns to go.*]
AIDE-DE-CAMP	Who are you? And who the hell asked your opinion?
OLUNDE	You're quite right, nobody. [*Going.*]
AIDE-DE-CAMP	What the hell! Did you hear me ask you who you were?
OLUNDE	I have business to attend to.
AIDE-DE-CAMP	I'll give you business in a moment you impudent nigger. Answer my question!
OLUNDE	I have a funeral to arrange. Excuse me. [*Going.*]
AIDE-DE-CAMP	I said stop! Orderly!

Ti-Jean and His Brothers

by Derek Walcott

Cast

(in order of appearance)

    Old Man / Devil

    Ti-Jean

    Mother

    Devils

    Chorus

    Bolom (Foetus)

    Frog

    Cricket

    Firefly

    Bird

    Brother 1

    Brother 2

8+ Speaking parts. Doubling is possible.

The Setting

The scene, which occurs in Scene 3 of this play, takes place in the late 1700's at dawn in a forest on the Caribbean island of St Lucia, during a period known as the Brigand War slave rebellion. Christian crosses mark the deaths of the brothers, 'Gros-Jean' and 'Mi-Jean'. There is a log and a hut belonging to Ti-Jean's Mother.

The Extract

The white Planter from the sugar cane plantation, is the Devil in disguise. Ti-Jean works for the Planter. His brothers are already dead, eaten by the Devil and, Ti-Jean is also in danger of being tricked and eaten by the Devil. In this scene the Planter / Devil is disguised as an Old Man. The text is in French and English and the scene uses song and dance as well as spoken text.

Scene 3

[*Dawn. The forest. Two crosses marked 'Gros Jean,' 'Mi-Jean.' The old man sits on the log, the creatures huddle near him. TI-JEAN, MOTHER, in the hut.*]

DEVILS   [*Off*] *Bai Diàble-la manger un 'ti mamaille,*
Un, deux, trois 'ti mamaille!
Bai Diàble-la manger un 'ti mamaille,
Un, deux, trois 'ti mamaille.

OLD MAN   Aie! Feed the Devil the third, feed the Devil the third. Power is knowledge, knowledge is power, and the Devil devours them on the hour!

DEVILS   *Bai Diàble-la manger un 'ti mamaille,*
Un, deux, trois 'ti mamaille!

OLD MAN   [*To audience*] Well, that's two good meals finished with a calm temper, and if all goes mortally, one more is to come. [*Shrieks, points to where TI-JEAN is consoling his MOTHER*] Aie, ya, yie, a chicken is to come, a calf, a veal-witted young man, tender in flesh, soft in the head and bones, tenderer than old muscle power, and simpler than that net-empty atheist. For the next dish is man-wit, commonsense. But I can wait, I can wait, gathering damp rotting faggots, aie!

MOTHER   [*To flute*] If you leave me, my son,
I have empty hands left,
Nothing to grieve for.
You are hardly a man,
A stalk, bending in wind
With no will of its own,
Never proven your self
In battle or in wisdom,
I have kept you to my breast,
As the last of my chickens,
Not to feed the blind jaws
Of the carnivorous grave.

TI-JEAN   You have told me yourself
Our lives are not ours,
That no one's life is theirs
Husband or wife,
Father or son,
That our life is God's own.

MOTHER	You are hard, hard, Ti-Jean, 0 what can I tell you? I have never learnt enough.
TI-JEAN	You have taught me this strength, To do whatever we will And love God is enough.
MOTHER	I feel I shall never see you again.
TI-JEAN	To return what we love is our glory, our pain.
OLD MAN	Oh, enough of these sentiments, I'm hungry, and I'm cold!
TI-JEAN	Now pray for me, maman, The sun is in the leaves.
MOTHER	The first of my children never asked for my strength, The second of my children Thought little of my knowledge, The last of my sons, now, Kneels down at my feet, Instinct be your shield, It is wiser than reason, Conscience be your cause And plain sense your sword,

[*The BOLOM rolls towards the hut. Drums*]

BOLOM	Old tree shaken of fruit, This green one must die.
MOTHER	Aie, I hear it, I hear it, The cry of the unborn! But then have I not given Birth and death to the dead?

[*The BOLOM dances off, shrieking. TI-JEAN rises.*]
Oh, Ti-Jean, you are so small,
So small. [*Exit*]

TI-JEAN	Yes, I small, maman, I small, And I never learn from book, But, like the small boy, David.

[*Sings*]

I go bring down, bring down Goliath,

Bring down below.
Bring down, bring down Goliath,
Bring down below.

[*He enters the forest*]

TI-JEAN   *Ah, bon matin, compere Crapaud,*
Still in your dressing-gown?

FROG   Ti-Jean, like your brothers you're making fun of me.

TI-JEAN   Why should I laugh at the frog and his fine bass voice?

FROG   You wouldn't call me handsome, would you?

TI-JEAN   [*Kneels among the creatures*]
Oh, I don't know, you have your own beauty.
Like the Castanet music of the cricket over there.

CRICKET   Crak, crak. Now say something nice to the firefly.

FIREFLY   How can he? I don't look so hot in the daytime.

TI-JEAN   But I have often mistaken you at night for a star.

[*Rises*] Now friends, which way is shortest to the Devil's estate?

FROG   Beware of an old man whose name is wordly wisdom.

FIREFLY   With a pile of sticks on his back.

CRICKET   ...and a foot cloven like a beast.

TI-JEAN   If he is an old man, and mortal,
He will judge everything on earth
By his own sad experience.
God bless you, small things.
It's a hard life you have.
Living in the forest.

FIREFLY   God preserve you for that.
Bird, take the tree and cry
If the old man comes through
That grove of dry bamboo.

[*BIRD flies off.*]

CRICKET   Crashing through the thicket
With the cleft hoof of a beast.

FIREFLY   For though we eat each other,
I can't tempt that frog too close,
And we never see each other for dinner,
We do not do it from evil.

FROG	True. Is a long time I never eat a firefly.
FIREFLY	Watch it, watch it, brother, You don't want heartburn, do you?
TI-JEAN	No, it is not from evil. What are these crosses?
CRICKET	Nothing. Do not look. Ti-Jean. Why must you fight the Devil?
TI-JEAN	To know evil early, life will be simpler.
FROG	Not so, Ti-Jean, not so. Go back.
	[*TI-JEAN goes to the crosses, weeps.*]
BIRD	Weep-weep-weep-weep-quick, The old man is coming, quick.
FROG	If you need us, call us, brother, but You understand we must move.
	[*TI-JEAN stands over the crosses.*]
OLD MAN	Ah, good morning, youngster! It's a damp, mournful walk through the forest, isn't it, and only the cheep of a bird to warm one. Makes old bones creak. Now it's drizzling. Damn it.
TI-JEAN	*Bon jou, vieux cor'*, I find the world pleasant in the early light.
OLD MAN	They say, the people of the forest, when the sun and rain contend for mastery, they say that the Devil is beating his wife. Know what I say? I say it brings rheumatism, I don't believe in the Devil. Eighty-eight years, and never seen his face.
TI-JEAN	Could you, being behind it?
OLD MAN	Eh? Eh? I'm deaf, come nearer. Come here and shelter. Good. Some people find me ugly, monstrous ugly. Even the small insects sometimes. The snake moves from me, and this makes me sad. I was a woodsman once, but look now. I burn wood into ashes. Let me sit on this log awhile. To-bacco?
TI-JEAN	No, thanks, sir.
OLD MAN	Tell me, boy, is your father living? Or your mother perhaps? You look frail as an orphan.
TI-JEAN	I think nothing dies. My brothers are dead but they live in the memory of my mother.

OLD MAN	You're very young, boy, to be talking so subtly. So you lost two brothers?
TI-JEAN	I said I had brothers, I never said how many. May I see that foot, father?
OLD MAN	In a while, in a while. No, I saw you looking at the two graves, so I presumed there were two. There were two, weren't there? Ah well, none can escape that evil that men call death.
TI-JEAN	Whatever God made, we must consider blessed. I'm going to look at your foot.
OLD MAN	Hold on, son. Whatever God made, we must consider blessed? Like the death of your mother?
TI-JEAN	Like the death of my mother.
OLD MAN	Like the vileness of the frog?
TI-JEAN	[*Advancing*] Like the vileness of the frog.
OLD MAN	Like the froth of the constrictor?
TI-JEAN	Like the froth of the constrictor. [*He is above the OLD MAN.*]
OLD MAN	Like the cloven cow's foot under an old man's skirt? [*TI-JEAN sweeps up the skirt, then drops it.*]
	What did you hope to find, but an old man's weary feet? You're a forward little fool! Now, do you want some advice? Tell me how you'll face the Devil, and I'll give you advice.
TI-JEAN	O help me, my brothers, help me to win. [*He retreats to the crosses.*]
OLD MAN	Getting frightened, aren't you? Don't be a coward, son. I gather twigs all day, in the darkness of the forest, And never feared man nor beast these eighty-eight years. I think you owe me some sort of apology.
	[*The BIRD runs out and begins to peck at the rope, untying the faggots with his beak. The OLD MAN jumps up, enraged.*]
	Leave that alone, you damned...
TI-JEAN	I'll help you, father.
	[*Instead, he loosens the bundle.*]
OLD MAN	I'll kill that bird. Why did you loosen my sticks? Haven't you any respect for the weariness of the old? You've had your little prank, now help me collect them. If you had a father you'd know what hard work was, In the dark of the forest, lighting damp faggots...

[*TI-JEAN pretends to be assisting the OLD MAN, but carefully he lifts his skirt and sees that below the sackcloth robe he has a forked tail.*]

TI-JEAN My mother always told me, my spirits were too merry, Now, here we are, old father, all in one rotten bundle.

OLD MAN What's come over you, you were frightened a while back?

TI-JEAN Which way to the Devil? Oh, you've never seen him. Tell me, does the Devil wear a hard, stiff tail?

OLD MAN How would I know. [*Feels his rear, realizes*] Mm. Well, you go through that track, and you'll find a short-cut through the bamboo. It's a wet, leaf-rotting path, then you come to the springs of sulphur, where the damned souls are cooking...

TI-JEAN You sure you not lying?

OLD MAN It's too early in the morning to answer shallow questions, That's a fine hat you're wearing, so I'll bid you goodbye.

[*TI-JEAN lifts up a stick.*]

TI-JEAN Not until I know who you are, papa!
Look, I'm in a great hurry, or I'll brain you with this;
If evil exists, let it come forward.
Human, or beast, let me see it plain.

[*The stage darkens. Drums. The OLD MAN rises.*]

OLD MAN Very well then, look!

[*He unmasks the DEVIL's face. Howls, cymbals clash*]

DEVIL Had you not gotten me, fool,
I might have played the Old Man
In fairness to our bargain.
But this is no play, son.
For here is the Devil,
You asked for him early,
Impatient as the young.
Now remember our bargain,
The one who wastes his temper,
Will be eaten! Remember that!
Now, you will work!

TI-JEAN Cover your face, the wrinkled face of wisdom,
Twisted with memory of human pain,
Is easier to bear; this is like looking
At the blinding gaze of God.

DEVIL [*Replacing OLD MAN's mask, and changing*]
It is hard to distinguish us,
Combat to fair combat, then I cover my face.
And the sun comes out of the rain, and the clouds.
Now these are the conditions, and the work you must do.

TI-JEAN Wait, old man, if is anything stupid,
I don't have your patience, so you wasting time.

OLD MAN Then you must pay the penalty.
These are your orders
I have an ass of a goat
That will not stay tied.
I want you to catch it
Tonight before sundown.
Over hill and valley
Wherever it gallops.
Then tie it good and hard.
And if it escapes
You must catch it again
As often as it gets loose
You try as many times.
If you should lose your temper .   .   .

TI-JEAN Where the hell is this goat?

OLD MAN Over there by the...wait.
The fool has run off.
He won't last very long.

[*Exit TI-JEAN. The OLD MAN sits down, rocking back and forth with laughter. TI-JEAN runs back.*]

OLD MAN Finished already?

TI-JEAN That's right. Anything else?

OLD MAN Ahm. Yes, yes, yes. Best I've seen, though.
Now I want you to go down to the edge of the cane field...

[*The goat bleats.*] Looks like you didn't tie him?

TI-JEAN I tied the damned thing up.
Something is wrong here.
I tied the thing up properly.

[*The OLD MAN laughs. TI-JEAN runs off. The OLD MAN dances with joy. Goat bleats, then stops suddenly. TI-JEAN returns with something wrapped in a banana leaf and sits down quietly. The OLD MAN watches him. Pause. No bleat.]*

OLD MAN   What's that in your hands?

TI-JEAN   [*Proffers the leaf*] Goat seed.

[*The goat bleats girlishly.*]

OLD MAN   His voice is changing.
I don't get you. Goat-seed?

TI-JEAN   I tied the damn thing. Then made it a eunuch.

[*The goat bleats weakly.*] Sounds much nicer.

OLD MAN   You er... fixed my one goat? Then you must have been angry.

TI-JEAN   No, I just couldn't see myself
Chasing the damned thing all night.
And anyhow, where I tied it,
She'll never move again.

OLD MAN   [*Walking around stage*]
You sit there calm as hell
And tell me you er... altered Emilia?

TI-JEAN   Funny goat, with a girl's name,
It's there by the plantain tree,
Just by the stones.

OLD MAN   Boy, you have a hell of a nerve.

TI-JEAN   It look like you vex.

OLD MAN   Angry? I'm not angry. I'm not vexed at all.
You see? Look! I'm smiling.
What's an old goat anyhow?
Just the only goat I had.
Gave sour milk anyway.

TI-JEAN   [*Rising. Rubbing his hands*] Fine. Now, what's next on the agenda?

OLD MAN   What? Yes, yes...fixed the goat...

TI-JEAN   Now look here, life is...

OLD MAN   Enough of your catechism!

TI-JEAN   Temper, temper. Or you might lose something. Now what next?

OLD MAN   Now, listen to this, boy.

Go down to the cane-fields
And before the next cloud
Start checking every blade.
Count each leaf on the stalk,
File them away properly
As fast as you can
Before the night comes,
Then report back to me.
Well, what are you waiting for?

TI-JEAN   I got a bit tired chasing the goat, I'm human you know.

OLD MAN   I'm going back to the house,

I'll be back at dawn to check on your progress. [*Exit*]

TI-JEAN   [*Goes to the edge of the cane-field*] Count all the canes, what a waste of time! [*Cups his hands*]
Hey, all you niggers sweating there in the canes!
Hey, all you people working hard in the fields!

VOICES   [*Far off*] 'Ayti? What happen? What you calling us for?

TI-JEAN   You are poor damned souls working for the Devil?

VOICES   Yes! Yes! What you want?

TI-JEAN   Listen, I'm the new foreman! Listen to this
The Devil say you must burn everything, now.
Burn the cane, burn the cotton! Burn everything now!

VOICES   Burn everything now? Okay, boss!

[*Drums. Cries. Caneburners' CHORUS*]

TI-JEAN   The man say Burn, burn, burn de cane!

CHORUS   Burn, burn, burn de cane!

TI-JEAN   You tired work for de man in vain!

CHORUS   Burn, burn, burn de cane!

[*Exeunt*]

[*The FROG enters.*]

FROG   [*Sings*]

And all night the night burned
Turning on its spit,
Until in the valley, the grid
Of the canefield glowed like coals,
When the devil, as lit as the dawn returned,

Dead drunk, and singing his song of lost souls.

[*Enter DEVIL, drunk, with a bottle, singing*]

DEVIL   Down deep in hell, where it black like ink,
Where de oil does boil and the sulphur stink,
It ain't have no ice, no refrigerator
If you want water, and you ask the waiter,
He go bring brimstone with a saltpetre chaser,
While de devils bawling.

[*He is carrying the OLD MAN's mask. Now he puts it on*]

Oh, if only the little creatures of this world could understand, but they have no evil in them ... so how the hell can
they? [*The CRICKET passes.*] Cricket, cricket, it's the old
man.

CRICKET   Crek, crek, boo!

CHORUS   Fire one! Fire one
Till the place burn down,
Fire one! Fire one.

DEVIL   [*Flings the mask away*]

I'll be what I am, so to hell with you. I'll be what I am. I
drink, and I drink, and I feel nothing. Oh, I lack heart to
enjoy the brevity of the world! [*The FIREFLY passes, dancing*] Get out of my way, you burning backside, I'm the prince
of obscurity and I won't brook interruption! Trying to
mislead me, because I been drinking. Behave, behave. That
youngster is having terrible effect on me. Since he came to
the estate, I've felt like a fool. First time in me life too. Look,
just a while ago I nearly got angry at an insect that's just a
half-arsed imitation of a star. It's wonderful! An insect
brushes my dragonish hand, and my scales tighten with
fear. Delightful! So this is what it means! I'm drunk, and
hungry. [*The FROG, his eyes gleaming, hops across his path*]
O God, O God, a monster! Jesus, help! Now that for one
second was the knowledge of death. O Christ, how weary it
is to be immortal. [*Sits down on log*] Another drink for
confidence.

[*Sings*]

When I was the Son of the Morning,

When I was the Prince of Light.

[*He picks up the mask.*]

Oh, to hell with that! You lose a job, you lose a job. Ambition. Yet we were one light once up there, the old man and I, till even today some can't tell us apart.

[*He holds the mask up. Sings*]

And so I fell for forty days,
Passing the stars in the endless pit.

Come here, frog, I'll give you a blessing. [*The FROG hops back, hissing.*] Why do you spit at me? Oh, nobody loves me, nobody loves me. No children of my own, no worries of my own. To hell with...[*Stands*] To hell with every stinking one of you, fish, flesh, fowl... I had the only love of God once [*Sits*] but I lost that, I lost even that.

[*Sings*]

Leaning, leaning,
Leaning on the everlasting arms...

To hell with dependence and the second-lieutenancy! I had a host of burnished helmets once, and a forest of soldiery waited on my cough, on my very belch. Firefly, firefly, you have a bit of hell behind you, so light me home. [*Roars at the creatures*] Get out, get out, all of you...Oh, and yet this is fine, this is what they must call despondency, weakness. It's strange, but suddenly the world has got bright, I can see ahead of me and yet I hope to die. I can make out the leaves, and...wait, the boy's coming. Back into the Planter. [*Wears the PLANTER's mask*]

TI-JEAN	[*Enters, also with a bottle*] Oh, it's you. you're back late. Had a good dinner?
DEVIL	You nearly scared me. How long you been hiding there?
TI-JEAN	Oh, I just came through. Drunk as a fish.
DEVIL	Finished the work?
TI-JEAN	Yes, sir. All you told me. Cleaned the silver, made up the fifty rooms, skinned and ate curried goat for supper, and I had quite a bit of the wine.
DEVIL	Somehow I like you, little man. You have courage. Your brothers had it too, but you are somehow different. Curried goat?...
TI-JEAN	They began by doing what you suggested. Dangerous. So naturally when the whole thing tired them, they got angry with themselves. The one way to annoy you is rank disobedience. Curried goat, yes.

DEVIL	We'll discuss all that in the morning. I'm a little drunk, and I am particularly tired. A nice bathtub of coals, and a pair of cool sheets, and sleep. You win for tonight. Tomorrow I'll think of something. Show me the way to go home.
TI-JEAN	[*His arms around the DEVIL*]

Oh, show me the way to go home,
I'm tired and I want to go to bed,
I had a little drink half an hour ago...

DEVIL	[*Removing his arm*] Wait a minute, wait a minute... I don't smell liquor on you. What were you drinking?
TI-JEAN	Wine, wine. You know, suspicion will be the end of you. That's why you don't have friends.
DEVIL	You have a fine brain to be drunk. Listen, I'll help you. You must have a vice, just whisper it in my ear and I won't tell the old fellow with the big notebook.
TI-JEAN	[*Holds up bottle*] This is my weakness. Got another drink in there?
DEVIL	[*Passing the bottle*] This is powerful stuff, friend, liquid brimstone. May I call you friend?
TI-JEAN	You may, you may. I have pity for all power. That's why I love the old man with the windy beard. He never wastes it. He could finish you off, like that...
DEVIL	Let's not argue religion, son. Politics and religion... You know, I'll confess to you. You nearly had me vexed several times today.
TI-JEAN	How did my two brothers taste?
DEVIL	Oh, let's forget it! Tonight we're all friends. It gets dull in that big house. Sometimes I wish I couldn't have everything I wanted. He spoiled me, you know, when I was his bright, starry lieutenant. Gave me everything I desired. I was God's spoiled son. Result: ingratitude. But he had it coming to him. Drink deep, boy, and let's take a rest from argument. Sleep, that's what I want, a nice clean bed. Tired as hell. Tired as hell. And I'm getting what I suspect is a hell of a headache. [*A blaze, lightens the wood*] I think I'll be going up to the house. Why don't you come in, it's damp and cold out here. It's got suddenly bright. Is that fire?
TI-JEAN	Looks like fire, yes.
DEVIL	What do you think it is, friend?
TI-JEAN	I think it's your house.

DEVIL   I don't quite understand

TI-JEAN   Sit down. Have a drink. In fact, I'm pretty certain it's your home. I left a few things on fire in it.

DEVIL   It's the only house I had, boy.

TI-JEAN   My mother had three sons, she didn't get vexed. Why not smile and take a drink like a man?

DEVIL   [*Removing the planter's mask*]

What the hell do you think I care about your mother? The poor withered fool who thinks it's holy to be poor, who scraped her knees to the knuckle praying to an old beard that's been deaf since noise began? Or your two damned fools of brothers, the man of strength and the rhetorician? Come! Filambol Azaz! Cacarat! You've burnt property that belongs to me.

[*Assistant DEVILS appear and surround TI-JEAN.*]

TI-JEAN   You're not smiling, friend.

DEVIL   Smiling? You expect me to smile? Listen to him! [*The DEVILS laugh*] You share my liquor, eat out my 'fridge, treat you like a guest, tell you my troubles. I invite you to my house and you burn it!

TI-JEAN   [*Sings*] Who with the Devil tries to play fair,
Weaves the net of his own despair.
Oh, smile; what's a house between drunkards?

DEVIL   I've been watching you, you little nowhere nigger! You little squirt, you hackneyed cough between two immortalities, who do you think you are? You're dirt, and that's where you'll be when I'm finished with you. Burn my house, my receipts, all my papers, all my bloody triumphs.

TI-JEAN   [*To the DEVILS*] Does your master sound vexed to you?

DEVIL   Seize him!

[*The BOLOM enters and stands between TI-JEAN and the devil*]

BOLOM   Master, be fair!
He who would with the devil play fair,
Weaves the net of his own despair.
This shall be a magnificent ending
A supper cooked by lightning and thunder.

[*Raises fork*]

MOTHER [*In a white light in the hut*]

Have mercy on my son,
Protect him from fear,
Protect him from despair,
And if he must die,
Let him die as a man,
Even as your Own Son
Fought the Devil and died.

DEVIL I never keep bargains. Now, tell me, you little fool, if you aren't afraid.

TI-JEAN I'm as scared as Christ.

DEVIL Burnt my house, poisoned the devotion of my servants, small things all of them, dependent on me.

TI-JEAN You must now keep
Your part of the bargain.
You must restore
My brothers to life.

DEVIL What a waste, you know yourself I can never be destroyed.

They are dead. Dead, look!

[*The BROTHERS pass.*]
There are your two brothers,
In the agony where I put them,
One moaning from weakness,
Turning a mill-wheel
For the rest of his life,
The other blind as a bat,
Shrieking in doubt.

[*The two BROTHERS pass behind a red curtain of flame.*]

TI-JEAN O God.

DEVIL [*Laughing*] Seize him! Throw him into the fire.

TI-JEAN [*With a child's cry*] Mama!

DEVIL She can't hear you, boy.

TI-JEAN Well, then, you pay her what you owe me!

I make you laugh, and I make you vex,

That was the bet. You have to play fair.

DEVIL Who with the devil tries to play fair...

TI-JEAN   [*Angrily*] I say you vex and you lose, man! Gimme me
           money!

DEVIL   Go back, Bolom!

BOLOM   Yes, he seems vexed,
           But he shrieked with delight
           When a mother strangled me
           Before the world light.

DEVIL   Be grateful, you would have amounted to nothing, child, a
           man. You would have suffered and returned to dirt.

BOLOM   No, I would have known life, rain on my skin, sunlight on
           my forehead. Master, you have lost. Pay him! Reward him!

DEVIL   For cruelty's sake I could wish you were born. Very well
           then, Ti-Jean. Look there, towards the hut, what do you see?

TI-JEAN   I see my mother sleeping.

DEVIL   And look down at your feet,
           Falling here, like leaves,
           What do you see? Filling this vessel?

TI-JEAN   The shower of sovereigns,
           Just as you promised me.
           But something is wrong.
           Since when you play fair?

BOLOM   Look, look, there in the hut,
           Look there, Ti-Jean, the walls,
           The walls are glowing with gold.
           Ti-Jean, you can't see it?
           You have won, you have won!

TI-JEAN   It is only the golden
           Light of the sun, on
           My mother asleep.

           [*Light comes up on the hut.*]

DEVIL   Not asleep, but dying, Ti-Jean.
           But don't blame me for that.

TI-JEAN   Mama!

DEVIL   She cannot hear you, child.
           Now, can you still sing?

FROG   Sing, Ti-Jean, sing!
           Show him you could win!

Show him what a man is!
Sing Ti-Jean...Listen,
All around you, nature
Still singing. The frog's
Croak doesn't stop for the dead;
The cricket is still merry,
The bird still plays its lute,
Every dawn, little Ti-Jean...

TI-JEAN [*Sings, at first falteringly*]
To the door of breath you gave the key,
Thank you, Lord,
The door is open, and I step free,
Amen, Lord...
Cloud after cloud like a silver stair
My lost ones waiting to greet me there
With their silent faces, and starlit hair
Amen, Lord.

[*Weeps*]

DEVIL What is this cooling my face, washing it like a
Wind of morning. Tears! Tears! Then is this the
Magnificence I have heard of, of
Man, the chink in his armour, the destruction of the
Self? Is this the strange, strange wonder that is
Sorrow? You have earned your gift, Ti-Jean, ask!

BOLOM Ask him for my life! O God, I want all this
To happen to me!

TI-JEAN Is life you want, child?
You don't see what it bring?

BOLOM Yes, yes, Ti-Jean, life!

TI-JEAN Don't blame me when you suffering,
When you lose everything,
And when the time come
To put two cold coins
On your eyes. Sir, can you give him life.

DEVIL Just look!

BOLOM [*Being born*] I am born, I shall die! I am born, I shall die!
O the wonder, and pride of it! I shall be man!
Ti-Jean, my brother!

DEVIL	Farewell, little fool! Come, then,
	Stretch your wings and soar, pass over the fields
	Like the last shadow of night, imps, devils, bats,
	Eazaz, Beelzebub, Cacarat, soar! Quick, quick the sun!
	We shall meet again, Ti-Jean. You, and your new brother!
	The features will change, but the fight is still on.
	[*Exeunt*]
TI-JEAN	Come then, little brother. And you, little creatures.
	Ti-Jean must go on. Here's a bundle of sticks that
	Old wisdom has forgotten. Together they are strong,
	Apart, they are all rotten.
	God look after the wise, and look after the strong,
	But the fool in his folly will always live long.
	[*Sings*]
	Sunday morning I went to the chapel
	Ring down below!
	I met the devil with the book and the Bible.
	Ring down below!
	Ask him what he will have for dinner.
CHORUS	Ring down below!
TI-JEAN	Cricket leg and a frog with water.
CHORUS	Ring down below!
TI-JEAN	I leaving home and I have one mission!
CHORUS	Ring down below!
TI-JEAN	You come to me by your own decision.
CHORUS	Ring down below!
TI-JEAN	Down in hell you await your vision.
CHORUS	Ring down below!
TI-JEAN	I go bring down, bring down Goliath.
CHORUS	Bring down below!
	[*Exeunt. The creatures gather as before.*]
FROG	And so it was that Ti-Jean, a fool like all heroes, passed through the tangled opinions of this life, loosening the rotting faggots of knowledge from old men to bear them safely on his shoulder, brother met brother on his way, that God made him the clarity of the moon to lighten the doubt of all travellers through the shadowy wood of life. And bird, the rain is over, the moon is rising through the leaves. Messieurs, creek. Crack.

Sizwe Bansi is Dead

by Athol Fugard

CAST

(in order of appearance)

Buntu

Man (Sizwe Bansi)

Styles

3 Speaking parts. Buntu and Styles may be doubled.

The Setting

The scenes, which take place towards the end of the play, occur in a variety of locations in Sizwe Bansi's 1970's, working class, African township of New Brighton, Port Elizabeth, South Africa. Settings include: an alleyway at night, and Buntu's house, which has a table and two chairs. Styles's Photographic Studio is also included.

The Extract

The South African apartheid system of government at this time in the 1970's demands that all indigenous (black) Africans carry (reference) pass books at all times to prove their identity. Man (Sizwe) has a dead man's pass book in his hand at the start of the scene. He needs to change his identity and is frightened. In his frustration and fear Man has discarded most of his clothes just prior to the opening of the scene.

BUNTU	Let me see your book?
	[*Sizwe doesn't respond.*] Give me your book!
MAN	Are you a policeman now, Buntu?
BUNTU	Give me your bloody book, Sizwe!
MAN	[*Handing it over*] Take it, Buntu. Take this book and read it carefully, friend, and tell me what it says about me. Buntu, does that book tell you I'm a man?
	[*BUNTU studies the two books. Sizwe turns back to the audience.*]
	That bloody book...! People, do you know? No! Wherever you go ... it's that bloody book. You go to school, it goes too. Go to work, it goes too. Go to church and pray and sing lovely hymns, it sits there with you. Go to hospital to die, it lies there too!
	[*BUNTU has collected Sizwe's discarded clothing.*]
BUNTU	Come!
	[*BUNTU's house, as earlier. Table and two chairs. BUNTU pushes Sizwe down into a chair. Sizwe still muttering, starts to struggle back into his clothes. BUNTU opens the two reference books and places them side by side on the table. He produces a pot of glue, then very carefully tears out the photograph in each book. A dab of glue on the back of each and then Sizwe's goes back into Robert's book, and Robert's into Sizwe's. Sizwe watches this operation, at first uninterestedly, but then he realizes what BUNTU is up to, with growing alarm. When he is finished, BUNTU pushes the two books in front of Sizwe.*]
MAN	[*Shaking his head emphatically*]. Yo! Haai, haai. No, Buntu.
BUNTU	It's a chance.
MAN	*Haai, haai, haai ...*
BUNTU	It's your only chance!
MAN	No, Buntu! What's it mean? That me, Sizwe Bansi. . . .
BUNTU	Is dead.
MAN	I'm not dead, friend.
BUNTU	We burn this book ... [*Sizwe's original*]... and Sizwe Bansi disappears off the face of the earth.
MAN	What about the man we left lying in the alleyway?

BUNTU	Tomorrow the Flying Squad passes there and finds him. Check in his pockets ... no passbook. Mount Road Mortuary. After three days nobody has identified him. Pauper's Burial. Case closed.
MAN	And then?
BUNTU	Tomorrow I contact my friend Norman at Feltex. He's a boss-boy there. I tell him about another friend, Robert Zwelinzima, book in order, who's looking for a job. You roll up later, hand over the book to the white man. Who does Robert Zwelinzima look like? You ! Who gets the pay on Friday? You, man!
MAN	What about all that shit at the Labour Bureau, Buntu?
BUNTU	You don't have to go there. This chap had a work-seeker's permit, Sizwe. All you do is hand over the book to the white man. He checks at the Labour Bureau. They check with their big machine. 'Robert Zwelinzima has the right to be employed and stay in this town.'
MAN	I don't want to lose my name, Buntu.
BUNTU	You mean you don't want to lose your bloody passbook! You love it, hey?
MAN	Buntu, I cannot lose my name.
BUNTU	[*Leaving the table*] All right, I was only trying to help. As Robert Zwelinzima you could have stayed and worked in this town. As Sizwe Bansi...? Start walking, friend. King William's Town. Hundred and fifty miles. And don't waste any time! You've got to be there by yesterday. Hope you enjoy it.
MAN	Buntu...
BUNTU	Lots of scenery in a hundred and fifty miles.
MAN	Buntu!...
BUNTU	Maybe a better idea is just to wait until they pick you up. Save yourself all that walking. Into the train with the escort! Smart stuff, hey. Hope it's not too crowded though. Hell of a lot of people being kicked out, I hear.
MAN	Buntu!...
BUNTU	But once you're back! Sit down on the side of the road next to your pondok with your family... the whole Bansi clan on leave... for life! Hey, that sounds okay. Watching all the cars passing, and as you say, friend, cough your bloody lungs out with Ciskeian Independence.

MAN	[*Now really desperate*]. Buntu!
BUNTU	What you waiting for? Go!
MAN	Buntu.
BUNTU	What?
MAN	What about my wife, Nowetu?
BUNTU	What about her?
MAN	[*Maudlin tears*] Her loving husband, Siwze Bansi, is dead!
BUNTU	So what! She's going to marry a better man.
MAN	[*Bridling*] Who?
BUNTU	You... Robert Zwelinzima.
MAN	[*Thoroughly confused*] How can I marry my wife, Buntu?
BUNTU	Get her down here and I'll introduce you.
MAN	Don't make jokes, Buntu. Robert...Sizwe...I'm all mixed up. Who am I?
BUNTU	A fool who is not taking his chance.
MAN	And my children! Their father is Sizwe Bansi. They're registered at school under Bansi...
BUNTU	Are you really worried about your children, friend, or are you just worried about yourself and your bloody name? Wake up, man! Use that book and with your pay on Friday you'll have a real chance to do something for them. You've got to be there by yesterday. Hope you enjoy it.
MAN	I'm afraid. How do I get used to Robert? How do I live as another man's ghost?
BUNTU	Wasn't Sizwe Bansi a ghost?
MAN	No!
BUNTU	No? When the white man looked at you at the Labour Bureau what did he see? A man with dignity or a bloody passbook with an N.I. number? Isn't that a ghost? When the white man sees you walk down the street and calls out, 'Hey, John! Come here'... to you, Sizwe Bansi... isn't that a ghost? Or when his little child calls you 'Boy'... you a man, circumcised with a wife and four children... isn't that a ghost? Stop fooling yourself. All I'm saying is be a real ghost, if that is what they want, what they've turned us into. Spook them into hell, man!
	[*Sizwe is silenced. BUNTU realizes his words are beginning*

to reach the other man. He paces quietly, looking for his next move. He finds it.]

Suppose you try my plan. Friday. Roughcasting section at Feltex. Paytime. Line of men – non-skilled labourers. White man with the big box full of pay-packets. 'John Kani!' 'Yes, sir!' Pay-packet is handed over. 'Thank you, sir.'

Another one. [*BUNTU reads the name on an imaginary pay-packet.*] 'Winston Ntshona!' 'Yes, sir!' Pay-packet over. 'Thank you, sir!' Another one. 'Fats Bhokolane!' 'Hier is ek, my baas!' Pay-packet over. 'Dankie. my baas!' Another one. 'Robert Zwelinzima!'

[*No response from Sizwe.*] 'Robert Zwelinzima!'

MAN	Yes, sir.
BUNTU	[*Handing him the imaginary pay-packet*] Open it. Go on.

[*Takes back the packet, tears it open, empties its contents on the table, and counts it.*]

Five... ten... eleven... twelve... and ninety-nine cents. In your pocket!

[*BUNTU again paces quietly, leaving Sizwe to think. Eventually...*]

Saturday. Man in overalls, twelve rand ninety-nine cents in the back pocket, walking down Main Street looking for Sales House. Finds it and walks in. Salesman comes forward to meet him.

'I've come to buy a suit.' Salesman is very friendly. 'Certainly. Won't you take a seat. I'll get the forms. I'm sure you want to open an account, sir. Six months to pay. But first I'll need all your particulars.'

[*BUNTU has turned the table, with Sizwe on the other side, into the imaginary scene at Sales House.*]

BUNTU	[*Pencil poised, ready to fill in a form*] Your name, please, sir?
MAN	[*Playing along uncertainly*] Robert Zwelinzima.
BUNTU	[*Writing*] 'Robert Zwelinzima.' Address?
MAN	Fifty, Mapija Street.
BUNTU	Where do you work?
MAN	Feltex.
BUNTU	And how much do you get paid?

MAN	Twelve... twelve rand ninety-nine cents.
BUNTU	N.I. Number, please?
	[*Sizwe hesitates.*] Your Native Identity number please?
	[*Sizwe is still uncertain. BUNTU abandons the act and picks up Robert Zwelinzima's passbook. He reads out the number.*]
	N–I– 3– 8–1–1– 8 – 6 – 3.
	Burn that into your head, friend. You hear me? It's more important than your name.
	N.I. number... three...
MAN	Three.
BUNTU	Eight.
MAN	Eight.
BUNTU	One.
MAN	One.
BUNTU	One.
MAN	One.
BUNTU	Eight.
MAN	Eight.
BUNTU	Six.
MAN	Six.
BUNTU	Three.
MAN	Three.
BUNTU	Again. Three.
MAN	Three.
BUNTU	Eight.
MAN	Eight.
BUNTU	One.
MAN	One.
BUNTU	One.
MAN	One.
BUNTU	Eight.
MAN	Eight.
BUNTU	Six.

MAN	Six.
BUNTU	Three.
MAN	Three.
BUNTU	[*Picking up his pencil and returning to the role of the salesman*] N.I. number, please.
MAN	[*Pausing frequently, using his hands to remember*]. Three... eight... one... one... eight... six... three...
BUNTU	[*Abandoning the act*] Good boy.

[*He paces. Sizwe sits and waits.*]

Sunday. Man in a Sales House suit, hat on top, going to church. Hymn book and bible under the arm. Sits down in the front pew. Priest in the pulpit.

[*BUNTU jumps on to a chair in his new role. Sizwe kneels,*]

The Time has come!

MAN	Amen!
BUNTU	Pray, brothers and sisters... Pray... Now!
MAN	Amen.
BUNTU	The Lord wants to save you. Hand yourself over to him, while there is still time, while Jesus is still prepared to listen to you.
MAN	[*Carried away by what he is feeling*] Amen, Jesus!
BUNTU	Be careful, my brothers and sisters...
MAN	Hallelujah!
BUNTU	Be careful lest when the big day comes and the pages of the big book are turned, it is found that your name is missing. Repent before it is too late.
MAN	Hallelujah! Amen.
BUNTU	Will all those who have not yet handed in their names for membership of our burial society please remain behind. [*BUNTU leaves the pulpit and walks around with a register,*]

Name, please, sir? Number? Thank you.

Good afternoon, sister. Your name, please.

Address? Number? God bless you. [*He has reached Sizwe.*]

Your name, please, brother?

MAN	Robert Zwelinzima.

BUNTU	Address?
MAN	Fifty, Mapija Street.
BUNTU	N.I. number.
MAN	[*Again tremendous effort to remember*] Three... eight... one... one... eight... six... three...

[*They both relax.*]

BUNTU	[*After pacing for a few seconds*]. Same man leaving the church... walking down the street.

[*BUNTU acts out the role while Sizwe watches. He greets other members of the congregation.*]

'God bless you, Brother Bansi. May you always stay within the Lord's mercy.'

'Greetings, Brother Bansi. We welcome you into the flock of Jesus with happy spirits.'

'God bless you, Brother Bansi. Stay with the Lord, the Devil is strong.'

Suddenly...

[*BUNTU has moved to behind Sizwe. He grabs him roughly by the shoulder.*]

Police!

[*Sizwe stands up frightened. BUNTU watches him carefully.*]

No, man! Clean your face.

[*Sizwe adopts an impassive expression. BUNTU continues as the policeman.*]

What's your name?

MAN	Robert Zwelinzima.
BUNTU	Where do you work?
MAN	Feltex.
BUNTU	Book!

[*Sizwe hands over the book and waits while the policeman opens it. looks at the photograph, then Sizwe, and finally checks through its stamps and endorsements. While all this is going on Sizwe stands quietly, looking down at his feet, whistling under his breath. The book is finally handed back.*]

Okay.

[*Sizwe takes his book and sits down.*]

MAN   [*After a pause*] I'll try it, Buntu.

BUNTU   Of course you must, if you want to stay alive.

MAN   Yes, but Sizwe Bansi is dead.

BUNTU   What about Robert Zwelinzima then? That poor bastard I pissed on out there in the dark. So he's alive again. Bloody miracle, man.

Look, if someone was to offer me the things I wanted most in my life, the things that would make me, my wife, and my child happy, in exchange for the name Buntu... you think I wouldn't swop?

MAN   Are you sure, Buntu?

BUNTU   [*Examining the question seriously*] If there was just me... I mean, if I was alone, if I didn't have anyone to worry about or look after except myself... maybe then I'd be prepared to pay some sort of price for a little pride. But if I had a wife and four children wasting away their one and only life in the dust and poverty of Ciskerian Independence.. if I had four children waiting for me, their father, to do something about their lives... *ag*, no, Sizwe...

MAN   Robert, Buntu.

BUNTU   [*Angry*] All right! Robert, John, Athol, Winston... Shit on names, man! To hell with them if in exchange you can get a piece of bread for your stomach and a blanket in winter. Understand me, brother, I'm not saying that pride isn't a way for us. What I'm saying is shit on our pride if we only bluff ourselves that we are men.

Take your name back, Sizwe Bansi, if it's so important to you. But next time you hear a white man say 'John' to you, don't say 'Ja. Baas?' And next time the bloody white man says to you, a man, 'Boy, come here,' don't run to him and lick his arse like we all do. Face him and tell him : 'White man. I'm a Man!' *Ag kak*! We're bluffing ourselves. It's like my father's hat. Special hat, man! Carefully wrapped in plastic on top of the wardrobe in his room. God help the child who so much as touches it! Sunday it goes on his head, and a man, full of dignity, a man I respect, walks down the street. White man stops him: 'Come here, kaffir!' What does he do?

[*BUNTU whips the imaginary hat off his head and crumples it in his hands as he adopts a fawning, servile pose in front of the white man.*]

'What is it, Baas?'

If that is what you call pride, then shit on it! Take mine and give me food for my children.

[*Pause.*]

Look, brother, Robert Zwelinzima, that poor bastard out there in the alleyway, if there are ghosts, he is smiling tonight. He is here, with us, and he's saying: 'Good luck, Sizwe! I hope it works.' He's a brother, man.

MAN   For how long, Buntu?

BUNTU   How long? For as long as you can stay out of trouble. Trouble will mean police station, then fingerprints off to Pretoria to check on previous convictions...and when they do that... Siswe Bansi will live again and you will have had it.

MAN   Buntu, you know what you are saying? A black man stay out of trouble? Impossible, Buntu. Our skin is trouble.

BUNTU   [*Wearily*] You said you wanted to try.

MAN   And I will.

            [*BUNTU picks up his coat*] I'm tired... Robert. Good luck. See you tomorrow.

            [*Exit BUNTU. Sizwe picks up the passbook, looks at it for a long time, then puts it in his back pocket. He finds his walking-stick, newspaper, and pipe and moves downstage into a solitary light. He finishes the letter to his wife.*]

MAN   So Nowetu, for the time being my troubles are over. Christmas I come home. In the meantime Buntu is working a plan to get me a Lodger's Permit. If I get it, you and the children can come here and spend some days with me in Port Elizabeth. Spend the money I am sending you carefully. If all goes well I will send some more each week. I do not forget you, my dear wife.

            Your loving Husband, Sizwe Bansi.

            [*As he finishes the letter, Sizwe returns to the pose of the photo. Styles Photographic Studio. Styles is behind the camera.*]

STYLES   Hold it, Robert. Hold it just like that. Just one more. Now smile, Robert... Smile... Smile...

            [*Camera flash and blackout.*]

The Man, his Son and their Donkey (Rhythms of Life)

by Mercy Mirembe Ntangaare

CAST

(in order of appearance)

Man

Son

Donkey

Kalisa

Woman

Pastor

6 Speaking Parts. No doubling.

Donkey may be played by more than one person.

The Setting

The scenes, which occur in Scenes 3 and 4 of this One Act play, take place on hot afternoon on a road in Uganda, near the Man, his Son and his Donkey's village.

The Extract

In Scene 3 the Man, his Son and his Donkey are returning from market. The play is a fable and like many African plays it employs a mixture of animal and human figures to tell a story that has a message. The Man faces various demands from his household. His Son's school fees need paying and new clothes need to be bought. The Man's wife complains about how much work she has to do. The Man's neighbour, cattle–keeper Kalisa, sees the Man's Donkey carrying a heavy load of sisal sacks full of beans, groundnuts and peas to market. When the Donkey complains the Man decides to redistribute the load between himself and his Son. Kalisa forces the Man to carry the bigger part of the load. The Man meets a Pastor on the road who tells him to rely on God to supply his needs.

Scene 3: On the Road

[*The same day. Early in the afternoon. Looking wearily, sweaty and dispirited. MAN, SON and DONKEY are on their way back home. The Donkey snorts in turns. Soon, they come to where KALISA is grazing his cattle. They are walking slowly past him when he stops them.*]

KALISA   [*Calling*] Eh! What has happened? You've come back same as you went.

MAN   [*Wearily, heavily*] I've learnt something new. We are God's own sons. We are princes of heaven, and not slaves or beggars anymore. God loves us, and he has kept for us riches in heaven where no moth or man shall corrupt them. Do we then need to keep toiling like this?

KALISA   Musoke, you are going mad.

MAN   Why? What have I done?

KALISA   You're saying things that are not connected.

MAN   Go and read Psalms 127:2, and stop enslaving yourself. It is useless for us to work so hard from early morning late into the night, just for food! God blesses those he loves, even when they are asleep.

KALISA   It's a crazy world, I swear!

MAN   Ask him, Pastor Stephen. Didn't he pass by you here?

KALISA   He certainly did, going to eat like the prince of heaven that he is. But you very well know that God helps those who help themselves.

MAN   Then he is making a mistake.

KALISA   [*Shocked, shakes Man vigorously by the shoulders*]

Musoke! ... Musoke! Come back to life. Your son needs to go back to school. You need to eat, buy clothes to wear, and so on. How are you going to manage?

MAN   As simply as that, [*Mechanically to SON*] Son, let's go. This man doesn't understand. He wants me to keep bleeding from inside like a donkey, [*Moves a few steps forward, stops, turns, and looks at KALISA nonchalantly*] If a man of God tells me not to worry who am I to try to be wiser than God?

KALISA   I swear you'll live to regret your actions! Do your work when you still can. Otherwise, you'll have a difficult time in old age.

MAN	Just mind your own business.

[*DONKEY bays painfully.*]

KALISA	Poor animal! Suffering silently, just like the sacks strapped on its back. I swear, he will die of overwork very soon!
MAN	Is he supposed to live forever?

[*They move on. After some short distance, they meet the WOMAN neighbour.*]

WOMAN	What has happened? You've come back same as you went.
MAN	[*Flexed*] Everybody in the village is asking the same question. Don't you have anything else to say?
WOMAN	We may get cheated at the marketplace but we don't have to quarrel with the road, do we? Mwami Musoke, isn't it strange that you've come back the same way you went?
MAN	[*Mechanically*] We don't need to work anymore. We are princes of heaven. God will take care of us.
WOMAN	Strange. But God helps those who help themselves. Pastor Stephen is always preaching about that.
MAN	That can't be true. He is preaching a different gospel right now.
WOMAN	That can't be true. Things can't change just like that. According to God, those who don't work should not eat.
MAN	I used to believe in hard work until this morning when I met the priest.
WOMAN	Which priest?
MAN	Pastor Stephen. He never works or toils like us but God always takes care of him. He has never passed a day without eating. His wife and children are always happy.
WOMAN	That could be true. But what will you now tell your wife? I left her busy grinding millet grain to make you a special meal. She said you were returning from the market today with a new dress for her and probably a kilogramme of meat.
MAN	[*Stupefied*] In that case, we shall just eat the food and sleep. The pastor said we should go home and rest,
WOMAN	I don't understand you at all.
MAN	It's useless to work so hard, from morning till evening, working just for food. God loves us; and he blesses those he loves even when they are asleep. Psalms 127: 2.

WOMAN	You must be tired in the head, indeed. Go home and rest. After you've woken up you'll realize your mistake. Travellers on the road of life never retreat. They never return to where they were before except to correct a mistake. Life is a forward-looking journey.
MAN	My head is getting confused. Please, let me go.
WOMAN	As you wish. [*She moves on.*]

Scene 4 At Home

[*MAN, SON and DONKEY also move on. Soon, the trio reach home. Wife sits by a heap of freshly thrashed beans, with a flat, round-shaped reed woven tray that she uses to toss the beans slightly in the air to help sort the seeds from the chaff. On her left is a sisal sack half-filled with cleaned beans. MAN, SON, and DONKEY trudge on, up to her.*]

WIFE	[*Looks up. Notices DONKEY is still loaded with sacks as before*] What has happened? Didn't the market open today?
MAN	[*Mechanically, as if it is a recitation*] Don't worry yourself for nothing. It's useless for us to work so hard from early morning until late at night, anxiously working for food to eat. Things have changed. We are God's own children and princes of heaven. Our riches are kept for us up in Heaven where no man or woman shall reach to corrupt them.
WIFE	God help us! Somebody has bewitched my husband.
MAN	No dear. I am in full control of my life. That's a fact. We no longer need to work so hard. It doesn't pay.
WIFE	Where are we going to get all the money we need to pay his school fees and buy clothes?
MAN	God blesses those he loves even when they are asleep. Psalms 172: 7 Oh! Is it?... No. Psalms 127: 2. That's what it says.
WIFE	My dear husband! A sack of butterflies must have hatched inside your brain. I don't understand what you're saying.
MAN	Everybody thinks I am mad. But I know what I am saying. Why do we need to toil and sweat when everything is already set out for us? Our riches are kept for us up in Heaven.
WIFE	What if you don't go to heaven?
MAN	I've told you.

WIFE	Son, did you eat something strange on the way? Your father is not the man I've known all these years.
MAN	Are you still doubting me? Look at Pastor Stephen. He is a man of God. He never works or toils like us. But his family is always happy, and he has never passed a day without food. We even met him going for lunch at Kalibala's place.
WIFE	[*She thinks to herself for a moment, then, resolutely*]
	No. Something must be done. Women from the monkey clan don't give up that easily. I shan't tolerate a lazy husband. Brahim, turn that donkey round. You must go back and sell something at the market.
MAN	I am not going back.
WIFE	You're going back. Since we don't have slaves to do all the dirty work for us we must do it ourselves.
MAN	Woman! Don't forget that I am the man in this house. I know what is good for us, and I will make decisions as I want.
WIFE	You've heard me right. I'm not going to suffer silently like a sack anymore. You either do the work or bring in servants and donkeys to work for you.
MAN	You're asking for something from me. [*He plants his right foot firmly on the ground, stretches his arms forward, and folds up the arms of his shirt, in readiness for a fight.*]
WIFE	[*Picks a threshing stick to arm herself*] You may beat me up but you shall beat me for nothing. I've suffered silently enough already.
MAN	Let me teach you the meaning of suffering. [*He charges at her.*]
WIFE	[*Making an alarm, as she takes up her position*] Wo - loo - loo - lo! Uu uu u! He's killing me...Wo - loo - lo - loo! Help! ...
PASTOR	[*Running into the compound*] Wo - loo - lo - loo! Uu uu u! Musoke's house is on fire! Uu uu u! Help!... [*Stops for a moment, and regards MAN and WIFE seriously, in turns*] What's the matter with you?
WIFE	[*Accusing her husband*] He's going to kill me...
MAN	I've suffered because of her for a long time. Let me teach her how a woman should behave... [*Charges at her again*]

PASTOR   [*Rushes to separate them*] No. No. No. It's not entertaining at all to see old people like you quarrelling and fighting like chickens! You're not even ashamed to fight before your son. What sort of child do you expect to raise after this?

MAN   The government has given too much freedom to the women. It has spoilt them. How can she think of beating me, her very own husband?

PASTOR   Stop it! She's your wife and you're her husband. God joined you together to raise a family according to his will. What's making you fight? Where's the problem?

WIFE   He went to the market to sell the beans so we could get some money to pay for his fees and buy clothes.

PASTOR   True. I met him on the way this morning toiling under the sacks, as the boy tossed his arms around shamelessly.

WIFE   But he has come back empty handed, telling me that it's useless for us to work so hard because God blesses those he loves even when they are asleep.

MAN   Ask Pastor Stephen if it's not true. He has never passed a day without food, and his family is always happy because God gives him all he needs.

PASTOR   [*Very amused*] Ha ha ha! Ha ha ha! My friend, God helps those who help themselves. Brother! I've cast my nets very far and wide, and I catch lots of fish – sardines, tilapia, Nile perch, name it. They all dive into my net, just like that! Ha ha ha! Remember the parable of the three servants?

    [*He observes MAN for a moment.*] Matthew 25: 19-29. [*Then, he opens his Bible and reads:*] 'After a long time, their master returned from his trip and called them to give an account of how they had used the money. The servant to whom he had entrusted the five bags of gold said, 'Sir, you gave me five bags of gold to invest, and I have doubled the amount.' The master was full of praise. 'Well done, my good and faithful servant. You have been faithful in handling this small amount, so now I will give you many more responsibilities. Let's celebrate together!' Next came the servant who had received the two bags of gold, with a report, 'Sir, you gave me two bags of gold to invest, and I have doubled the amount.' The master said, 'Well done, my good and faithful servant. You have been faithful in handling this small amount, so now I will give you many more responsibilities. Let's celebrate together!' Then the servant with one bag of gold came and said, 'Sir, I know you are a hard man, harvesting crops you didn't plant and gathering crops you didn't cultivate. I was afraid I would lose your money, so I hid it in the earth and here it is.' But the master replied, 'You wicked and lazy servant! You think I am a hard man, do you, harvesting crops I didn't plant and gathering crops I didn't cultivate? Well, you should at least have put my money in the bank so I could have some interest. Take the money from this servant and give it to the one with ten bags of gold.' [*He closes his Bible and holds it securely under his left arm.*] That's the law of life. He he he! The person who has something will be given more, so that he will have more than enough; but the person who has nothing will have taken away from him even the little he has. He he he! My friend, work hard, when you still have strength in your bones. Time will come when you can do nothing for yourself.

[*There is a short, heavy silence.*]

SON | Pastor, our donkey works very hard. Will it also have its riches multiplied? Donkeys are our beasts of burden. They have no riches of their own.

PASTOR | But they have life and blood under their skins. That's true. But if you take a donkey away from work what shall it become?

MAN | They become lazy and useless. Just like the women.

PASTOR | Mwami Musoke, let's not open up another war front. Everything has a right to be. For the moment, it would make good sense for you to go back to the market, and try to sell something. Everybody must have some means of livelihood, however small or tough.

WIFE | He must also remember to buy my dress. I am not going to suffer and die silently like that donkey.

PASTOR | [*Looking at WIFE, in caution*] I said, let's not open up new war fronts, [*Turns to MAN*] Musoke, let's go.

[*MAN slaps the DONKEY very hard, to urge it to move. It bays painfully.*]

PASTOR | Soft, my friend. That donkey may be the beast of burden but, as the young man here says, it has life and blood under its skin.

[*Silence. MAN, SON, PASTOR and DONKEY move on, to the rhythm of life, till they disappear from sight.*]

End of the play

Glossary

Rudali

accha	okay
alta	decorative red dye for the feet used by married women
arre	alas
badis	a spicy concoction of dal (lentil) balls
bahu	daughter-in law
bhaiya	brother
black-tongued	speaking in a nasty way
Brahmans	priests who are highest in the caste hierarchy
chakki	two stones used for grinding wheat to make flour
charpoy	string bed
chivda	rice snack
daain	a witch who brings bad luck
Dushads	one of the lower sub-castes of Untouchables
Ganjus	one of the lower sub-castes of Untouchables
ghagra	skirt worn mostly by village women
Hai Maiyya	Oh Mother
Hanumanji	the Monkey God
Kriya	last death rites
Malik-mahajan	landlord
Mela	village market
Panchayat	council of elderly (wise) people
Panda	Brahmin holy person
peepul tree	rain tree
pinda	Offering of food for the spirits to eat.
Ram Bhagwan	Lord Ram
Ram!	Oh my God!
Rupee	Indian dollar
Sattu	mix of legumes, dal
Shivji Maharaj	priest
sindoor	vermillion coloured stripe which runs along central hair parting of a married woman
Thakur	second highest caste — landlord or warrior caste

Ka Shue

amah	nursemaid, female nanny
cheongsam	a fitting dress worn by women, generally made from silk.
daw geh	thank you
Guilo	foreign white devil
mahlee	(not a Cantonese word, broken English for "Marry")
Paw paw	maternal grandmother
till na ma	a Cantonese swear word or phrase that basically means "Go screw your mother!"

Death and the King's Horseman

alari	a rich, woven cloth, brightly woven
egungun	ancestral masquerade
etutu	placatory rites or medicine
gbedu	a deep-timbred royal drum
opele	string of beads used in of a divination

Sizwe Bansi is Dead

Baas	boss
Dankie	thank you
Ek	is
hier	here

Acknowledgements

Extract from *Ka Shue (Letters Home)* by Lynda Chanwai Earle. The Women's Play Press, 2003. Reprinted with permission from Playmarket, Wellington, New Zealand. All applications for a licence to perform the extract from the play should be addressed to the author's agent c/- Playmarket P.O.Box 9767, Te Aro, Wellington 6141, New Zealand. info@playmarket.org.nz

Extract from *Top Girls* by Caryl Churchill. Methuen Drama, 1991. Reprinted with permission from A & C Black Ltd., London. U.K. All applications for a licence to perform the extract from the play should be addressed to the author's agent c/- A & C Black A & C Black Ltd., 36 Soho Square, London W1D 3QY, U.K. www.acblack.com

Extract from *Cloudstreet* by Nick Enright, Justin Mojo and Tim Winton. Currency Press, 1999. Reprinted with permission from Currency Press Ltd., Strawberry Hills, NSW, Australia. All applications for a licence to perform the extract from the play should be addressed to the authors' agent c/- Currency Press Ltd., Strawberry Hills, NSW, 2010 Australia. enquiries@currency.com.au

Extract from *Sizwe Bansi is Dead* by Athol Fugard. In *Statements – Three Plays* . Oxford University Press, 1991, Oxford, U.K. Reprinted with permission of Oxford University Press, Oxford, U.K. All applications for a licence to perform the extract from the play should be addressed to the author's agent c/- William Morris Agency (U.K.) Ltd., or William Morris Agency Inc. N.Y. U.S.A.

Extract from *Leaving Home* by David French. House of Anansi Press, 2004. Reprinted with permission from House of Anansi Press Inc., Toronto, Canada. All applications for a licence to perform the extract from the play should be addressed to the author's agent c/- House of Anansi Inc. 110 Spadina Avenue, Suite 801 Toronto, ON M5V 2K4 Canada. www.anansi.ca

Extract from *Rudali* by Usha Ganguli. Translated into English from the original Hindi by Anjum Katyal. *Rudali*, based on Mahasweta Devi's short story of the same name, was adapted into a play by Usha Ganguli in 1992. First published by Seagull Books Private Limited, Calcutta, India, 1997. Reprint 1998, 2001, 2007, 2008. Translation copyright Seagull Books, 1997. All applications for a licence to perform the extract from the play should be addressed to the author. c/- Seagull Books Private Limited seagullfoundation.support@gmail.com

Extract from *Summer of the Seventeenth Doll* by Ray Lawler. Currency Press, 1978. Reprinted with permission from Currency Press Ltd., Strawberry Hills, NSW, Australia. All applications for a licence to perform the extract from the play should be addressed to the author's agent c/- Currency Press Ltd, Strawberry Hills, NSW, 2010 Australia. enquiries@currency.com.au

Extract from *The Pohutukawa Tree* by Bruce Mason. Price Milburn,1960. Wellington, New Zealand. Reprinted with permission from Playmarket, Wellington, New Zealand. All applications for a licence to perform the extract from the play should be addressed to the author's agent c/- Playmarket P.O.Box 9767, Te Aro, Wellington 6141, New Zealand. info@playmarket.org.nz

Extract from *The Man, His Son and their Donkey* by Mercy Mirembe Ntangaare. In *The Rat Trap and Other Plays*. 2007. MPK Graphics Ltd, Kampala, Uganda. All applications for a licence to perform the extract from the play should be addressed to the author's agent c/- MPK Graphics Ltd., PO Box 30596, Kampala, Uganda.

Extract from *An Inspector Calls* by J.B. Priestley. In *14 Great Plays*. William Heineman Limited, 1977. London, U.K. Reprinted with permission from Peters Fraser & Dunlop Group Ltd., (PFD) London, U.K. All applications for a licence to perform the extract from the play should be addressed to the author's agent c/- Peters Fraser & Dunlop Group Ltd., (PFD) Drury House   34-43 Russell Street , London, WC2B 5HA www.pfd.co.uk

Extract from *Death and the King's Horseman* by Wole Soyinka. Methuen, 1975. London, UK. Reprinted with permission from A & C Black Ltd., London. U.K. All applications for a licence to perform the extract from the play should be addressed to the author's agent c/- A & C Black A & C Black Ltd, 36 Soho Square, London W1D 3QY, U.K. www.acblack.com

Extract from *Atomic Jaya* by Huzir Sulaiman. In *Eight Plays* by Huzir Sulaiman, Silverfishbooks, 2002. Reprinted with permission from Silverfishbooks Kuala Lumpur, Malaysia. All applications for a licence to perform the extract from the play should be addressed to the author's representatives, Checkpoint Theatre, Singapore, at agent@checkpoint-theatre.org

Extract from *Ti-Jean and His Brothers* by Derek Walcott. In *Dream on Monkey Mountain: and Other Plays*. Farrar, Straus and Giroux, U.S.A. 1970. Reprinted with permission from Farrar, Straus & Giroux, New York, USA. All applications for a licence to perform the extract from the play should be addressed to the author's agent c/- Farrar, Straus & Giroux, 18 West 18th St, New York, NY 10011 USA